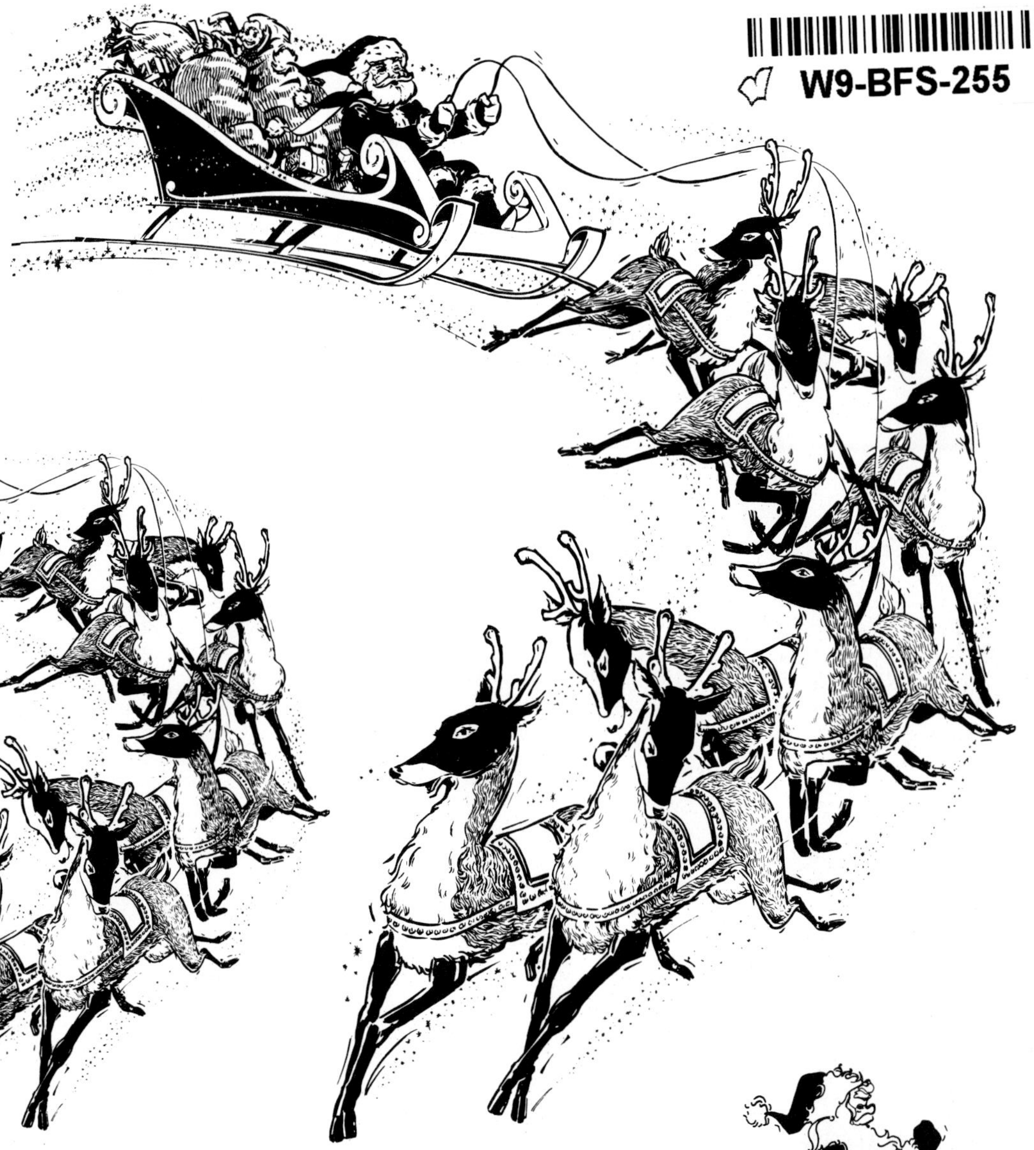

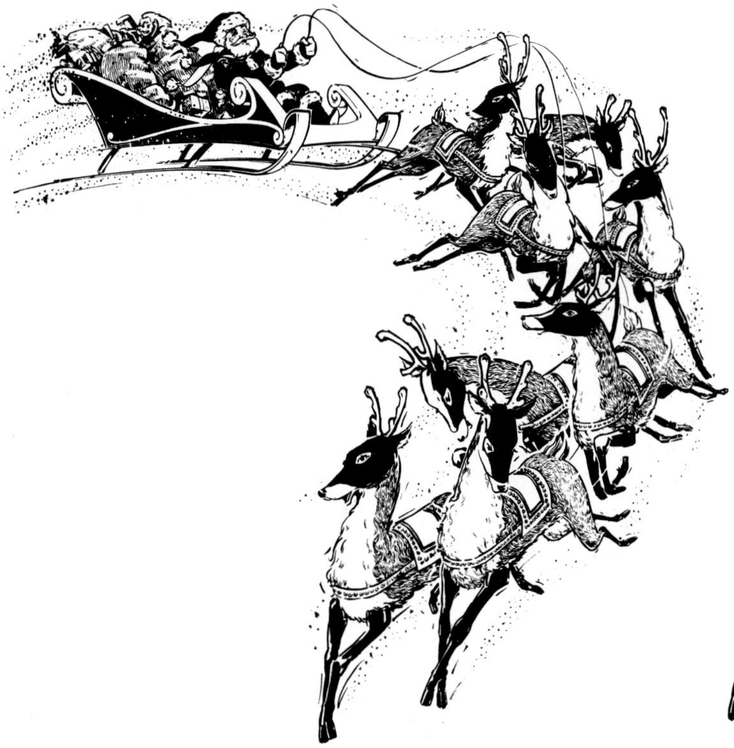

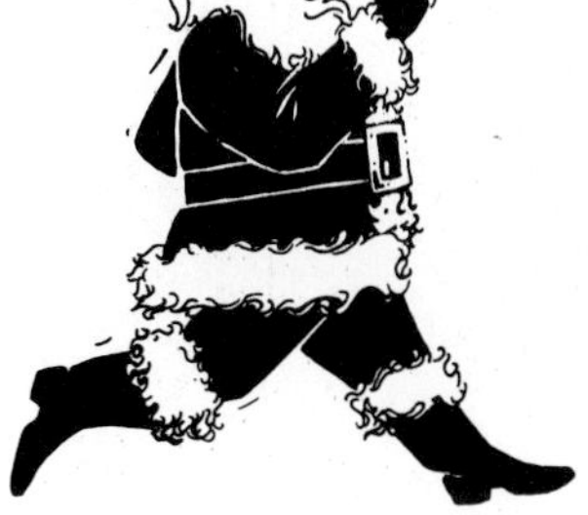

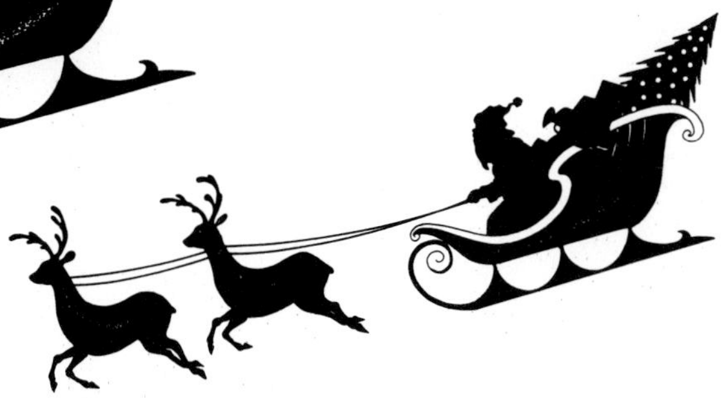

■ Characters

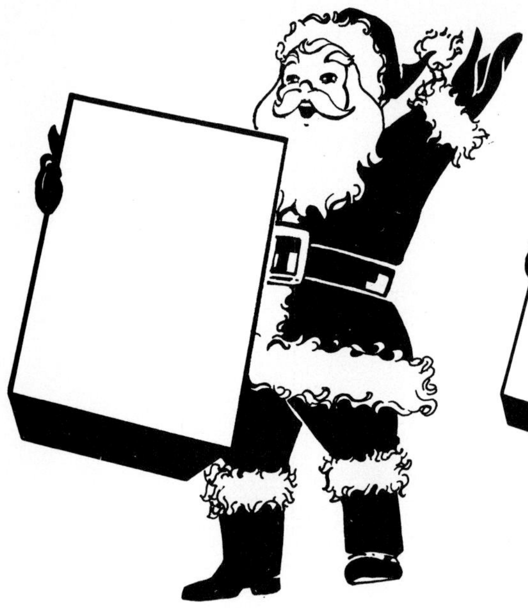

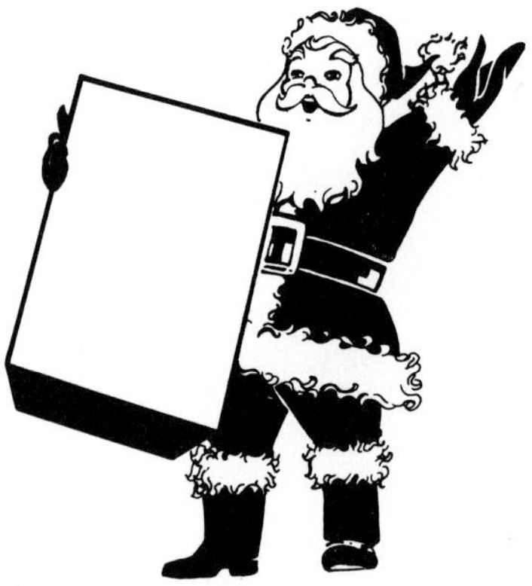

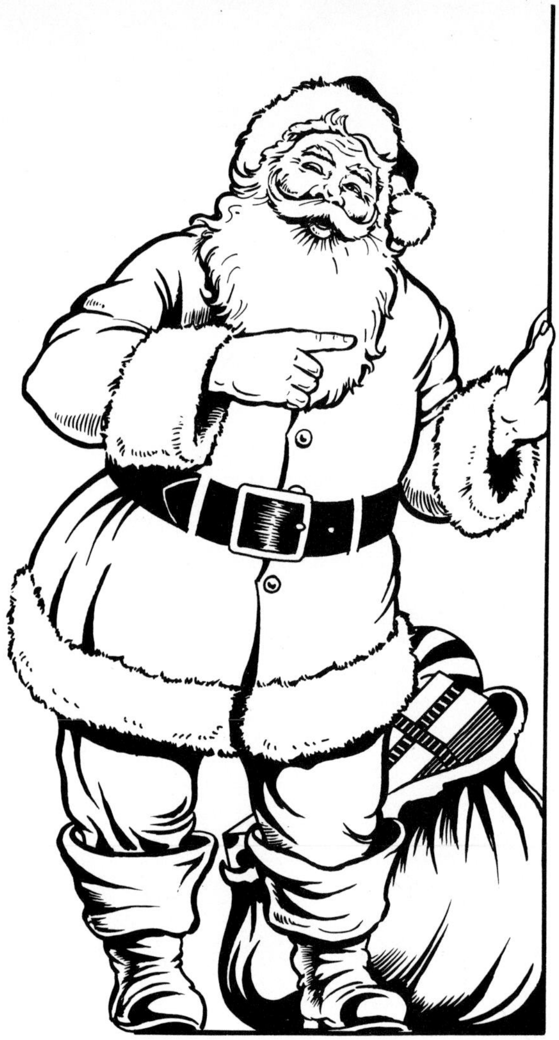

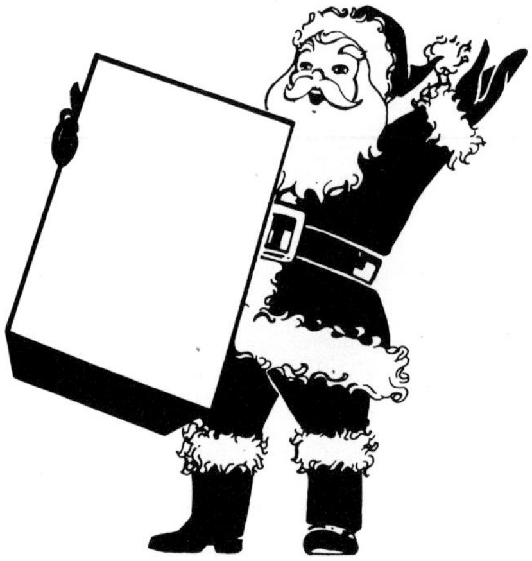

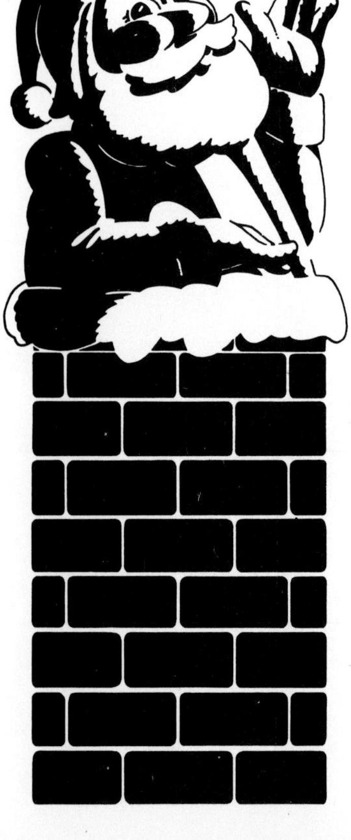

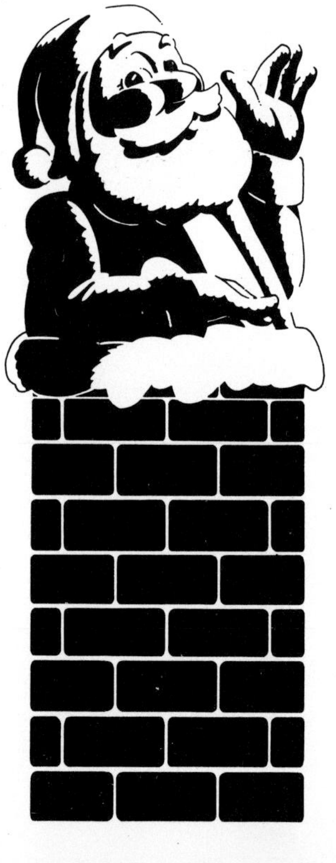

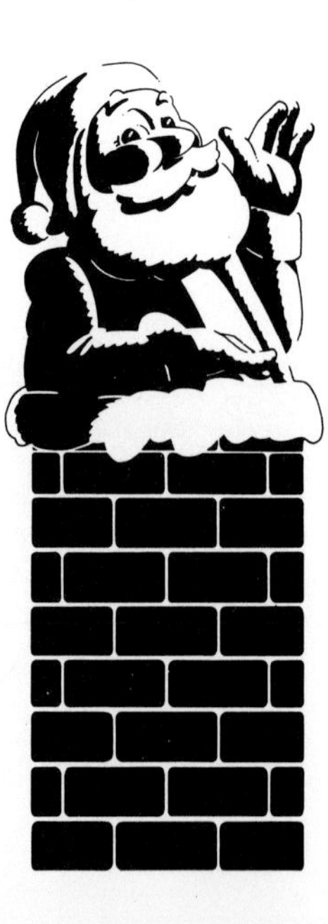

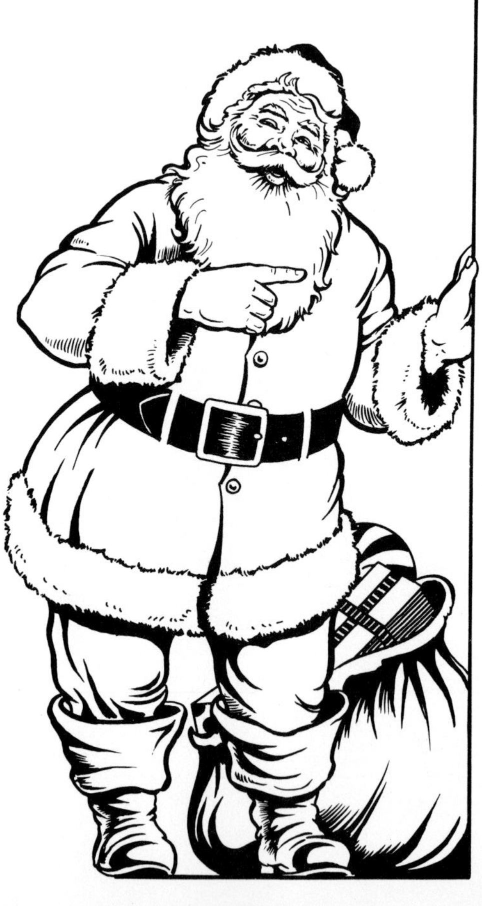

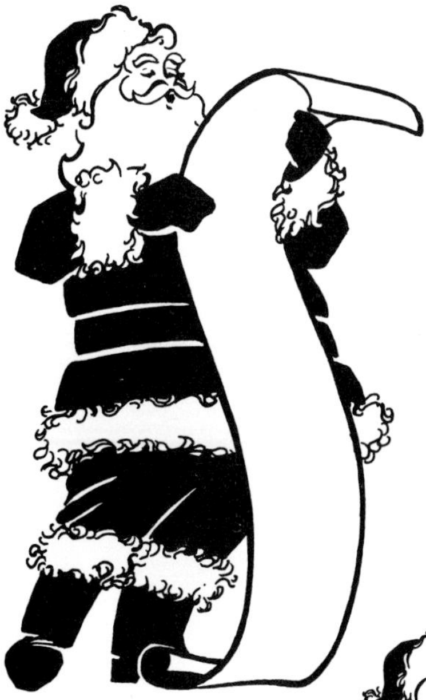

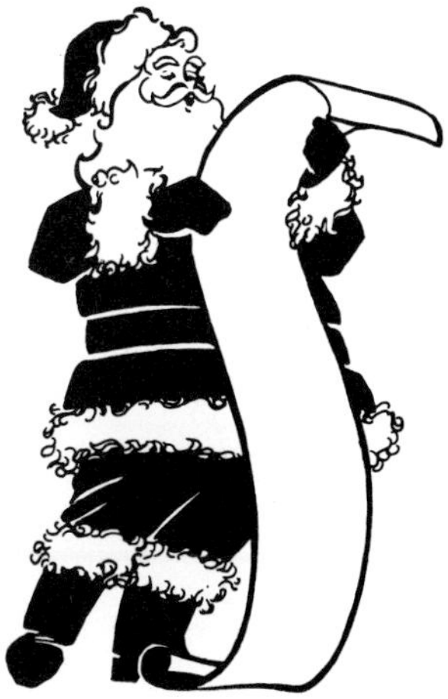

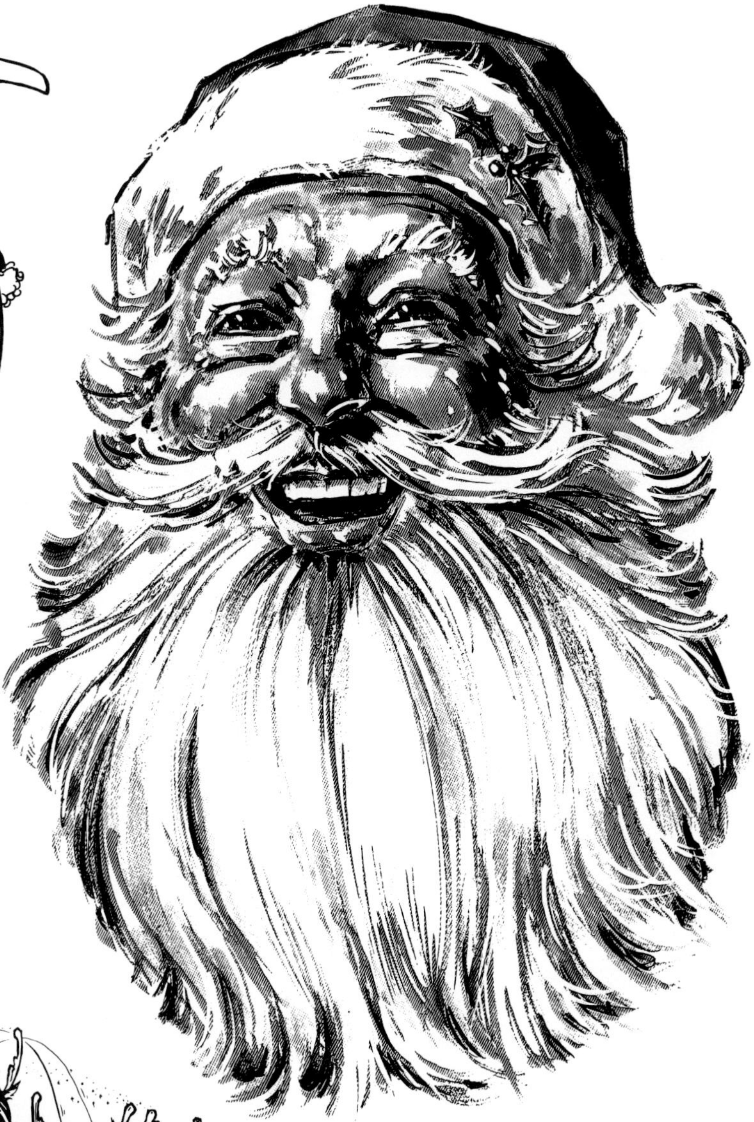

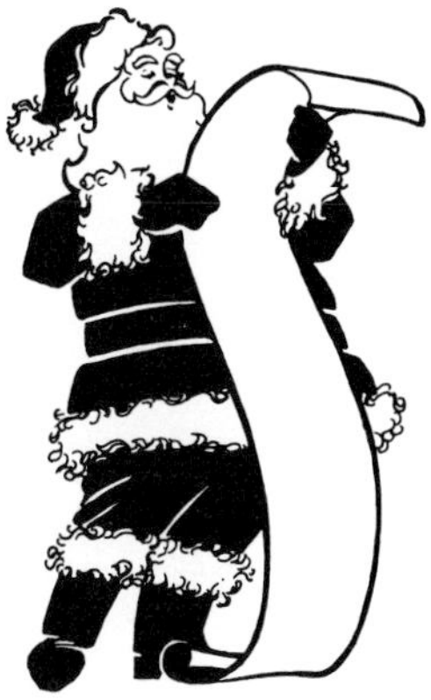

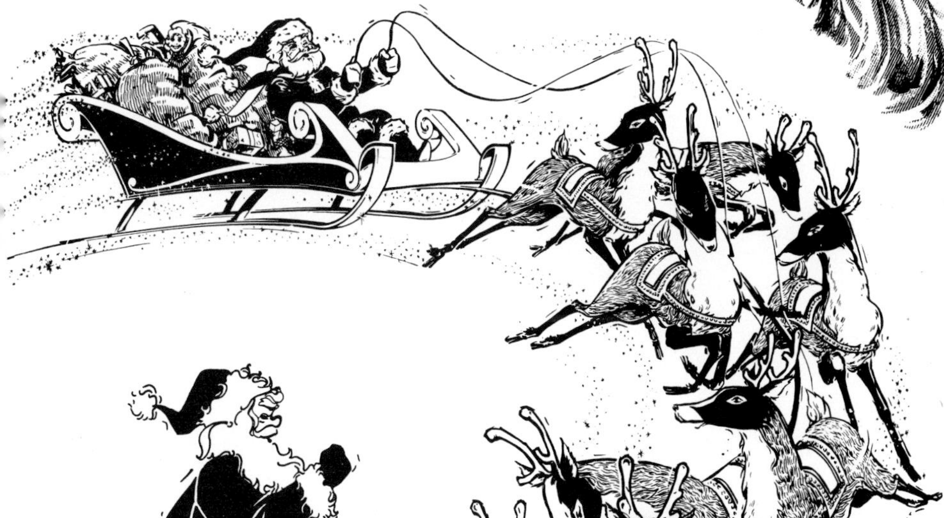

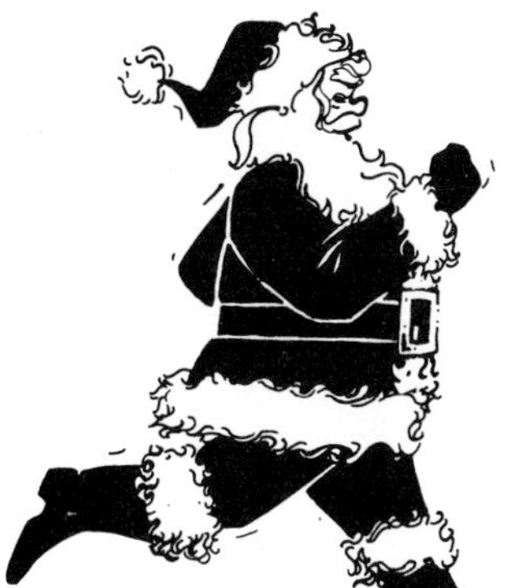

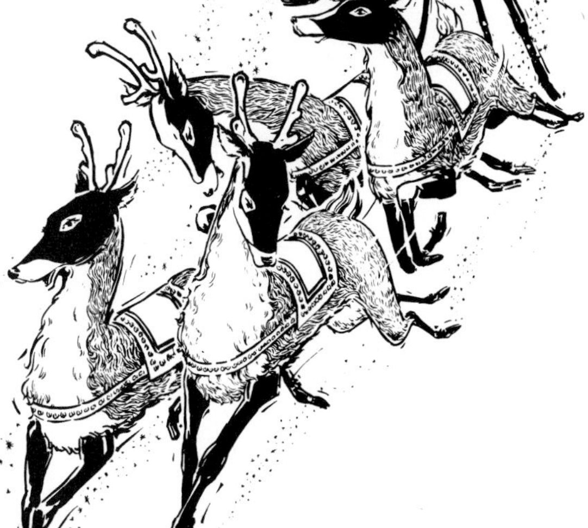

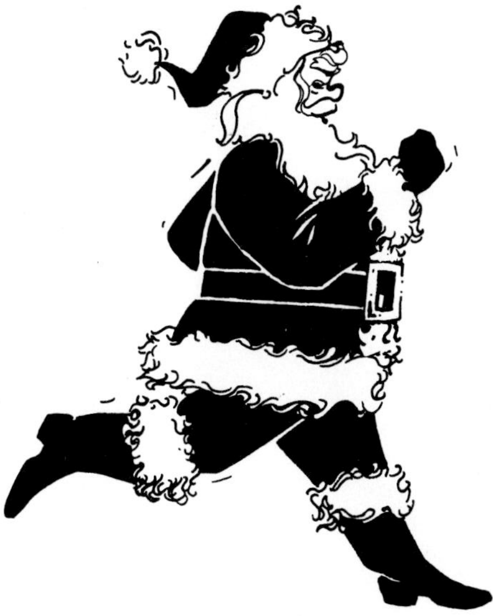

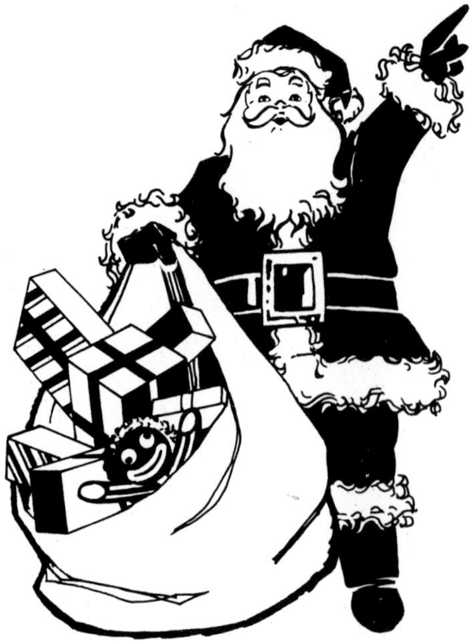

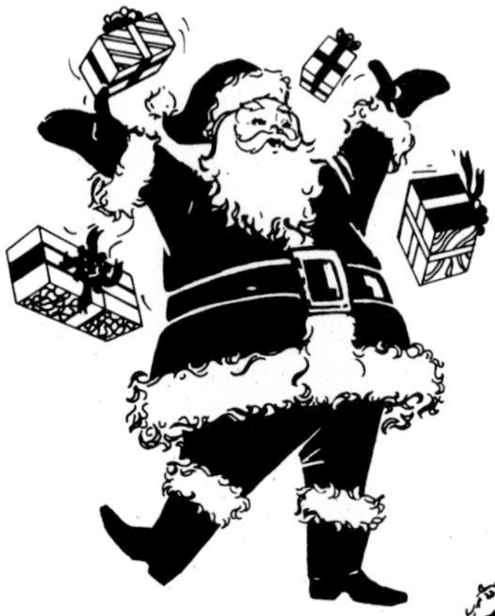

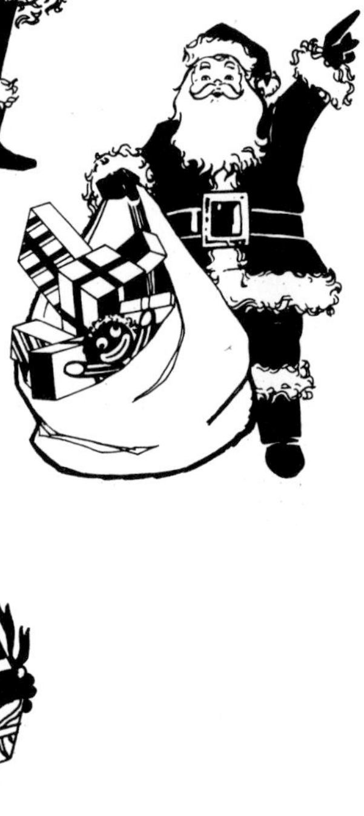

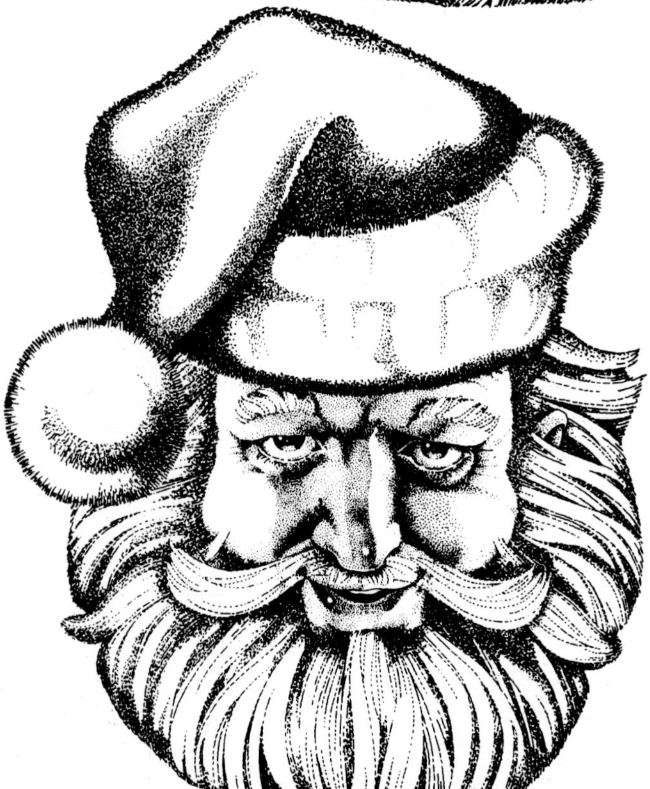

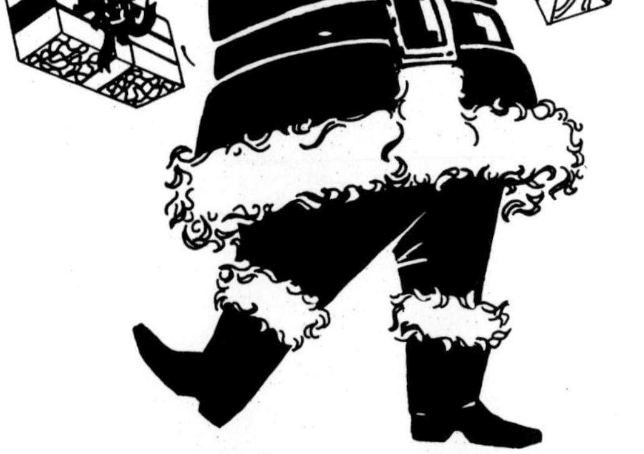

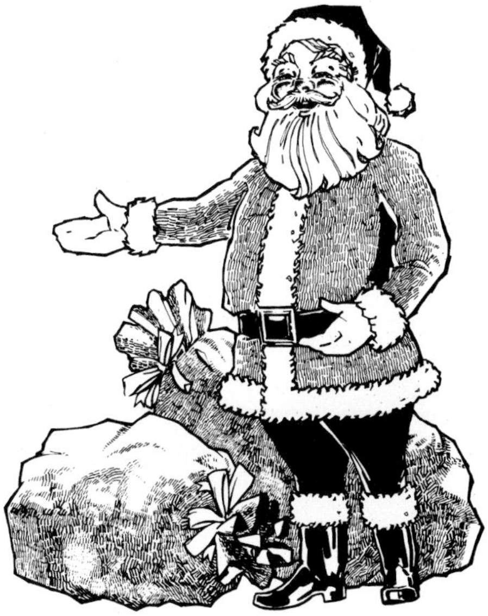

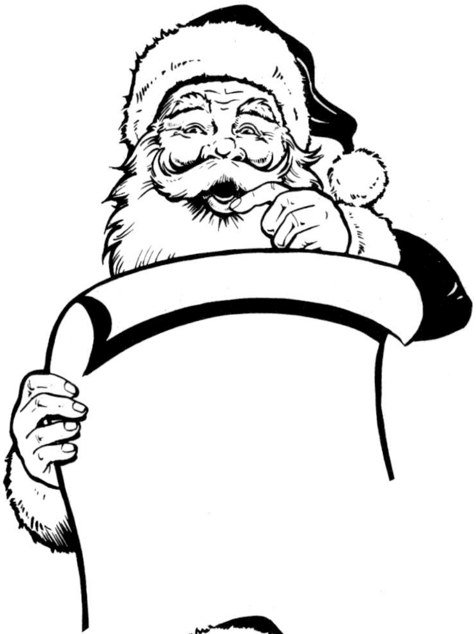

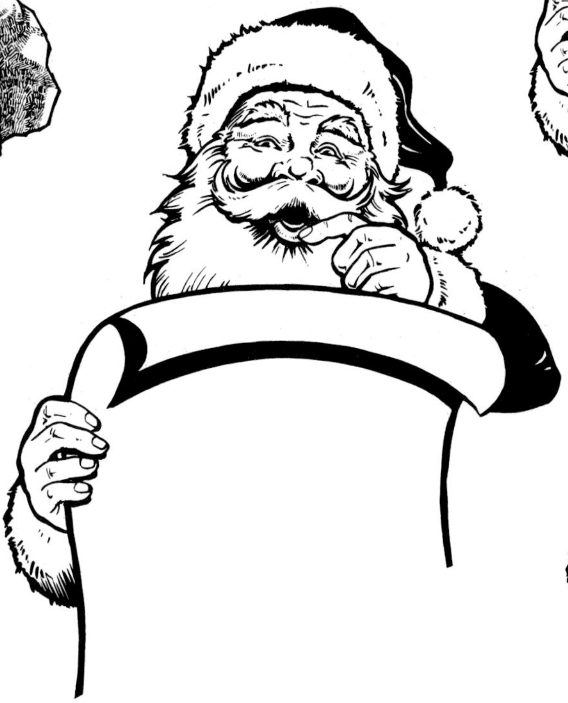

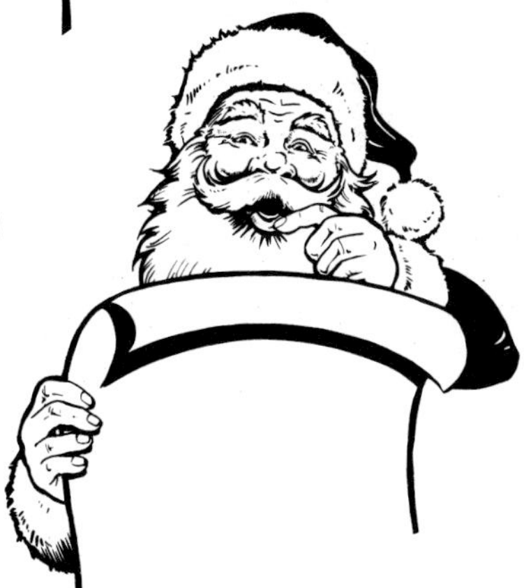

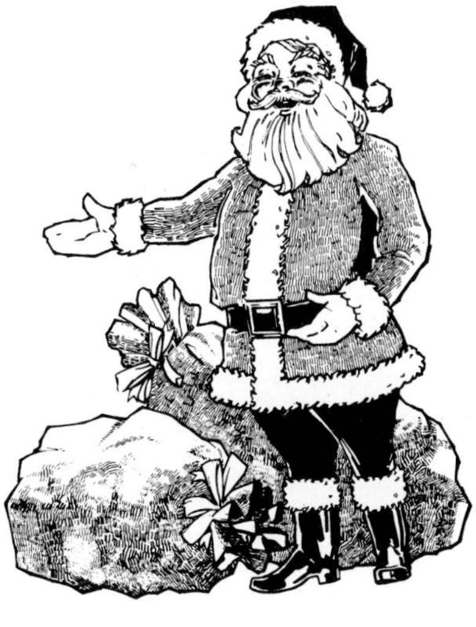

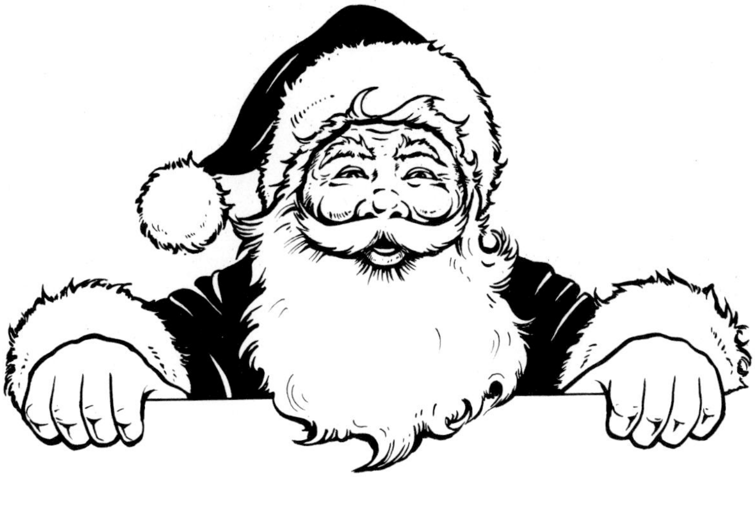

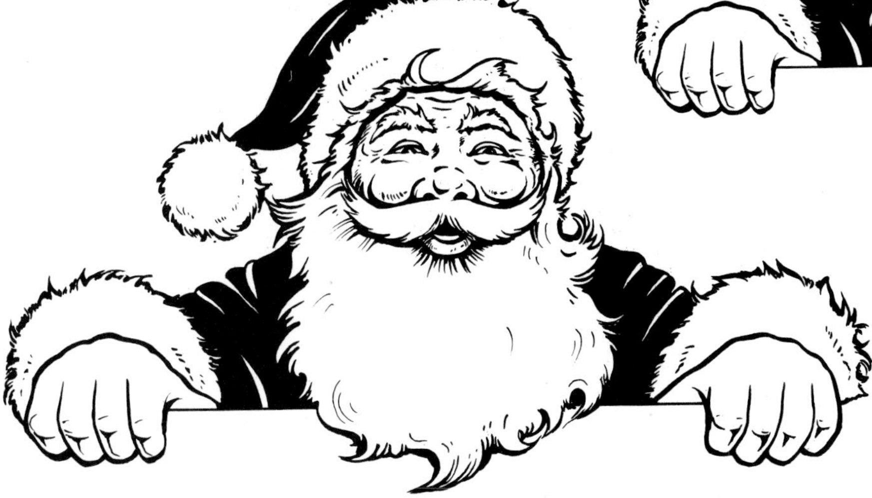

■ Characters

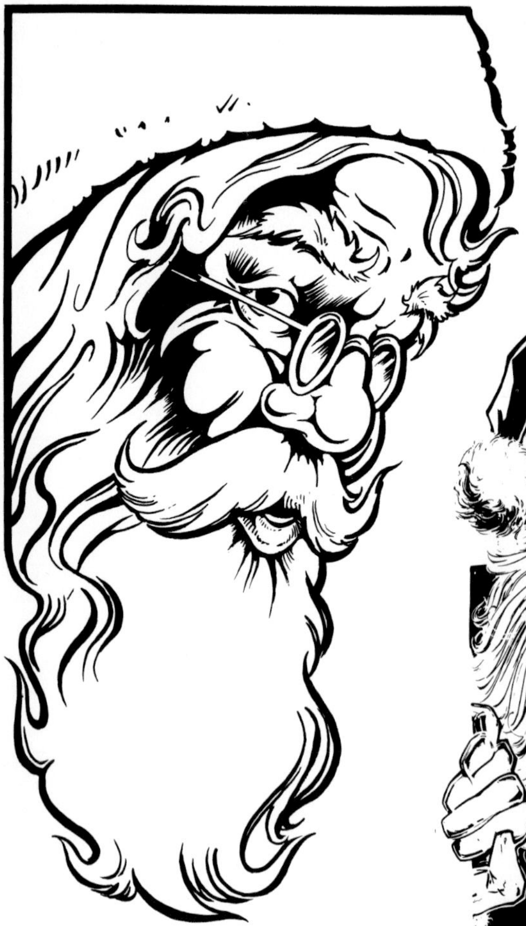

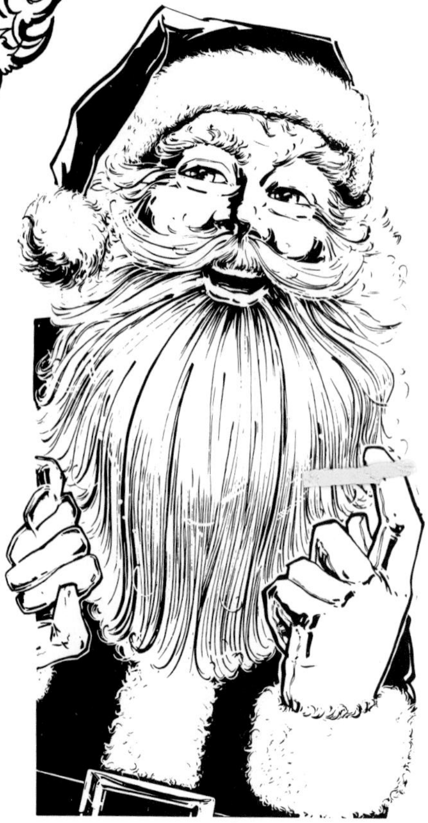

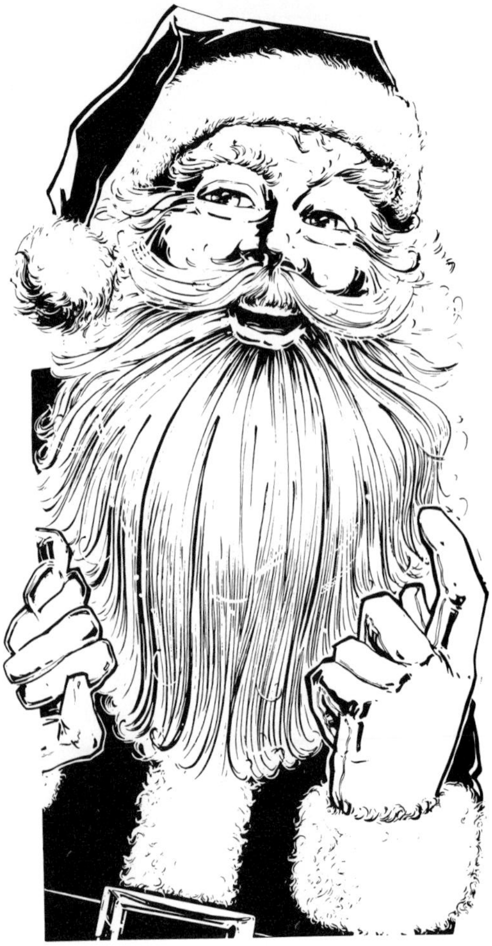

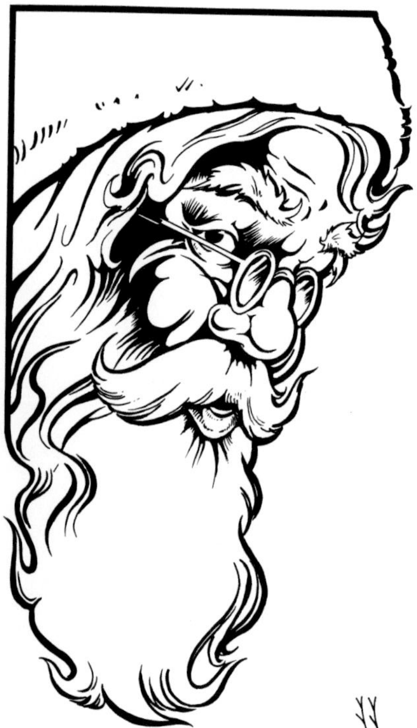

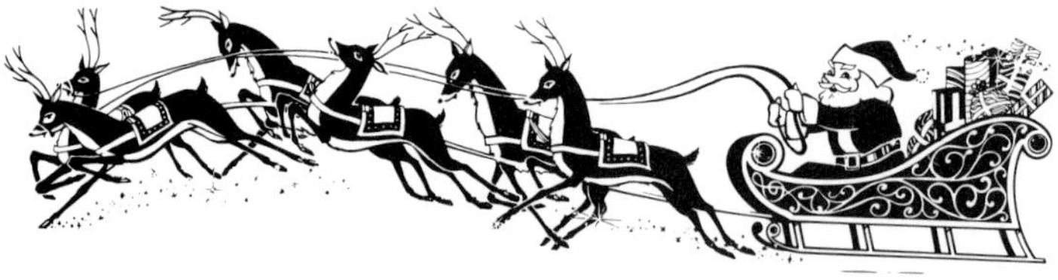

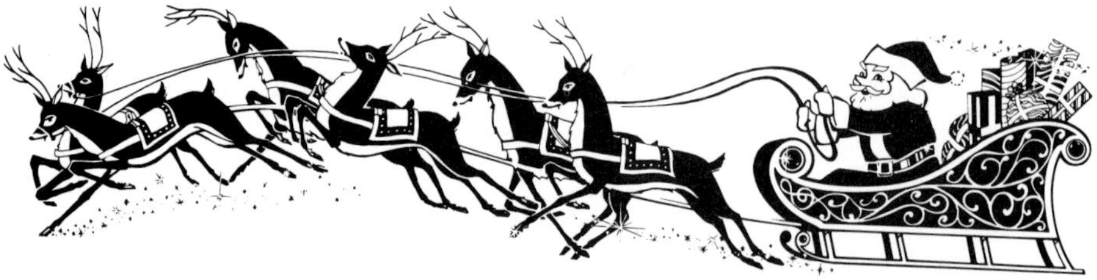

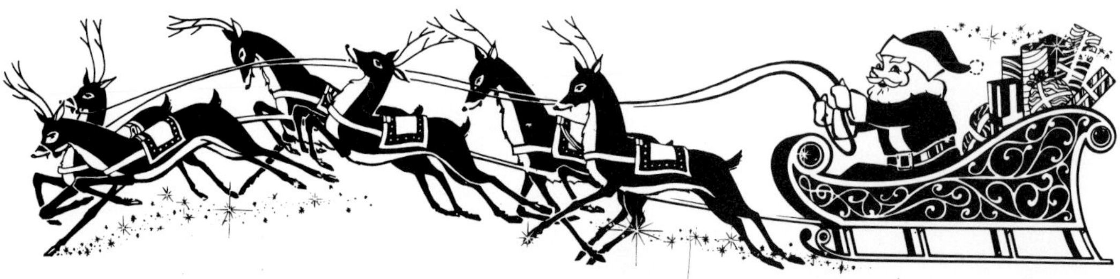

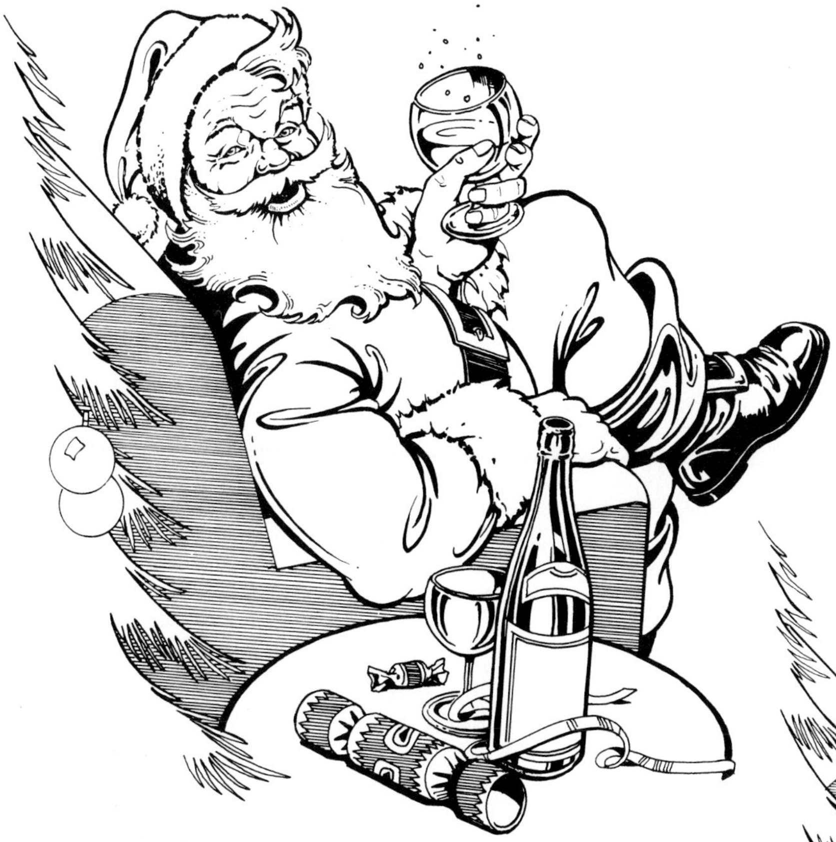

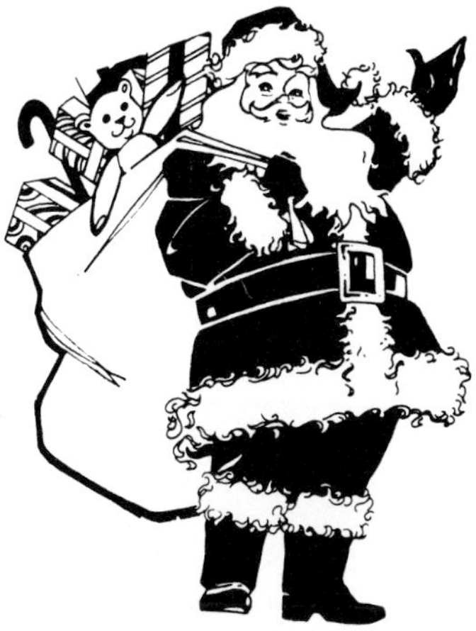

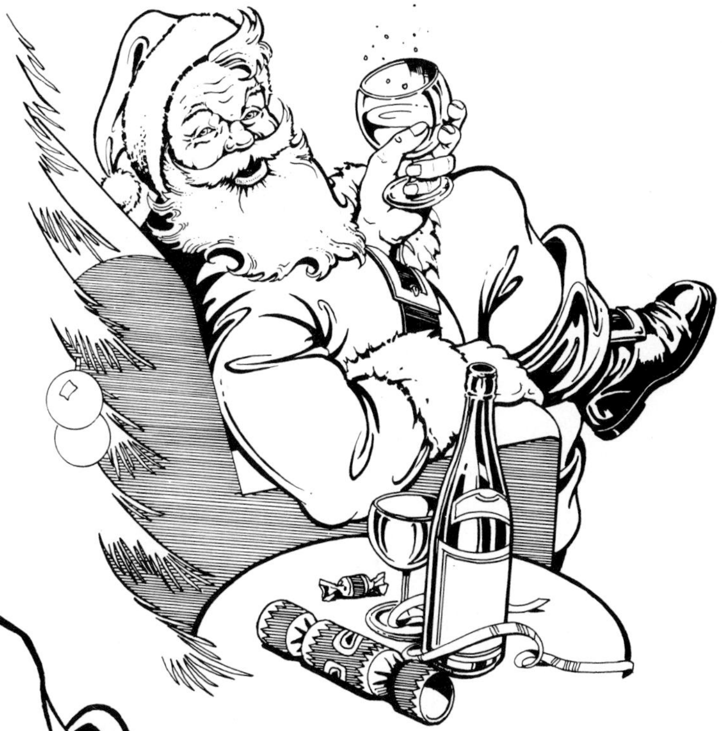

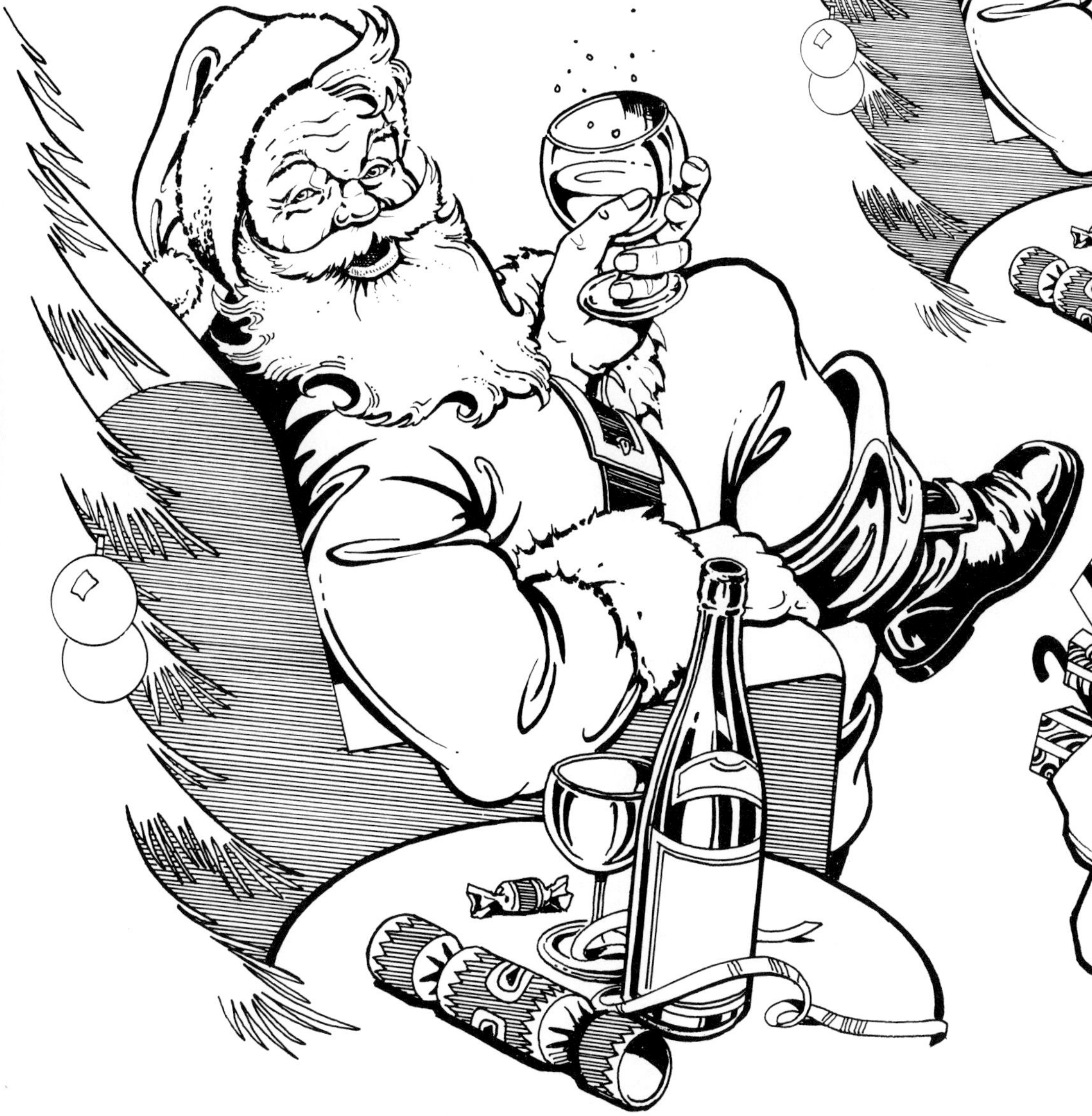

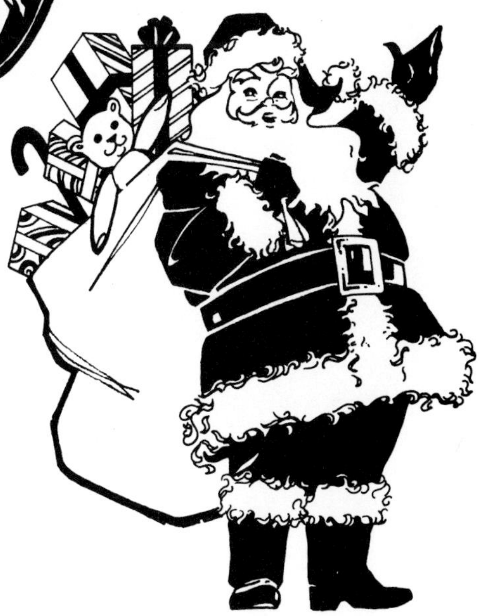

■ Characters

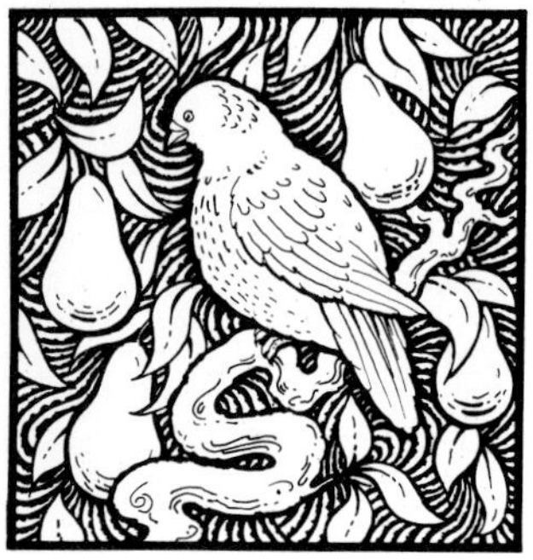

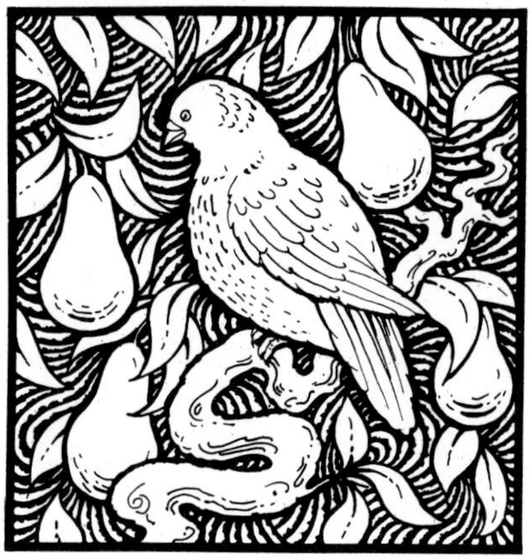

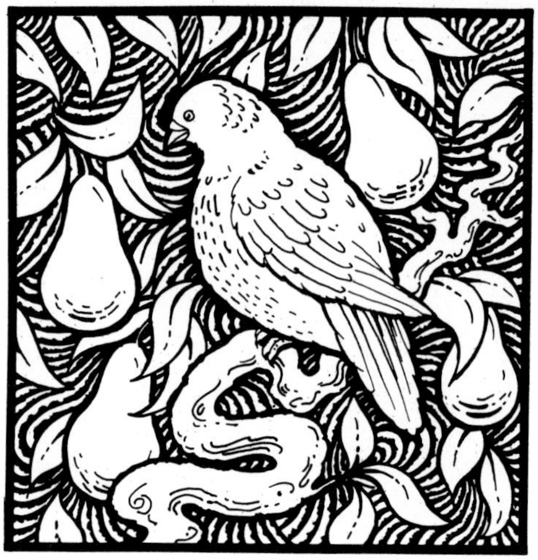

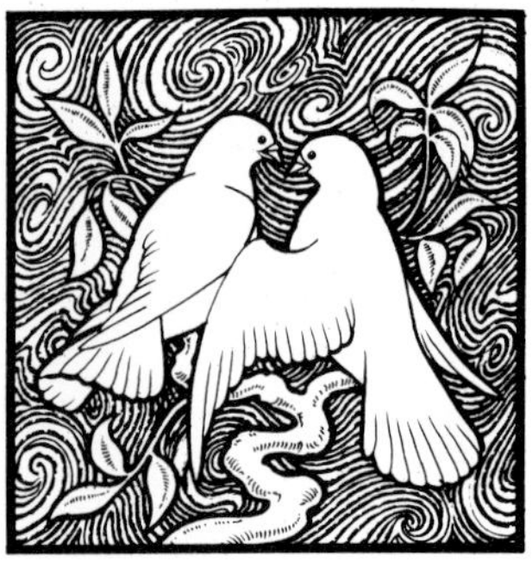

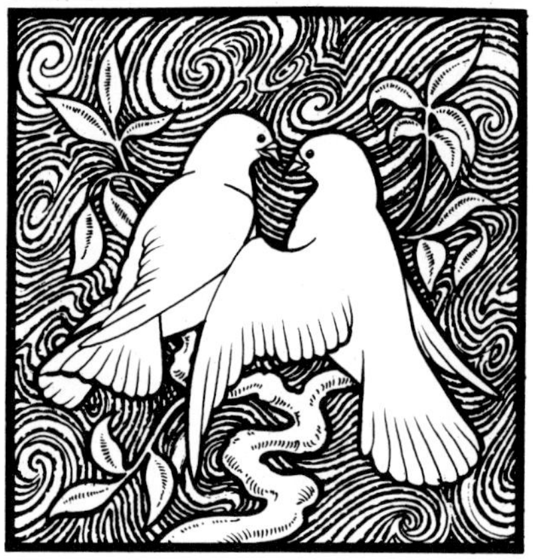

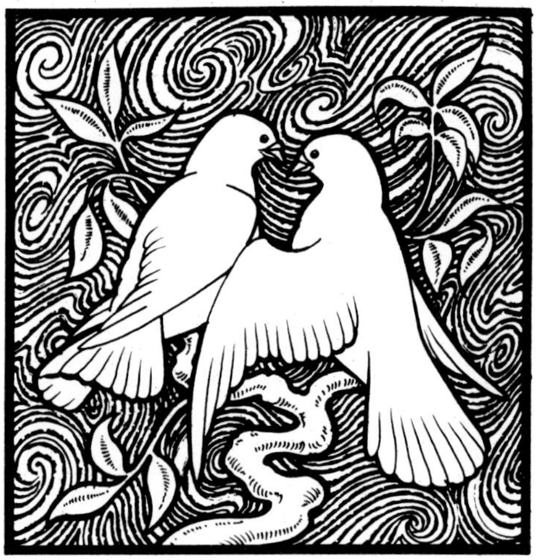

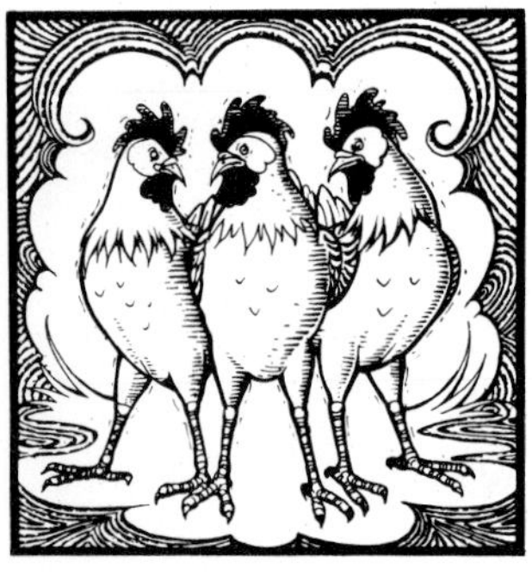

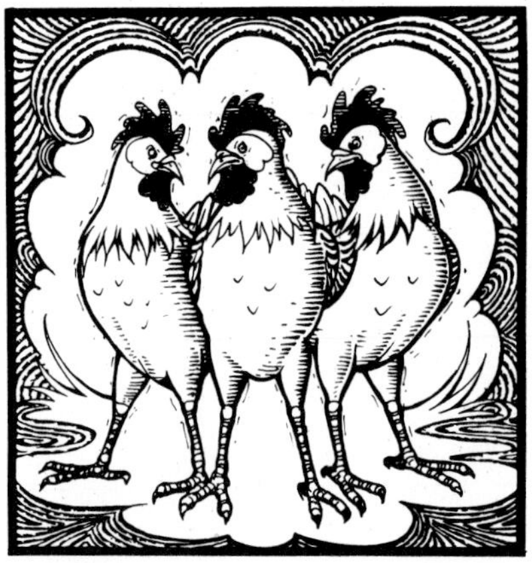

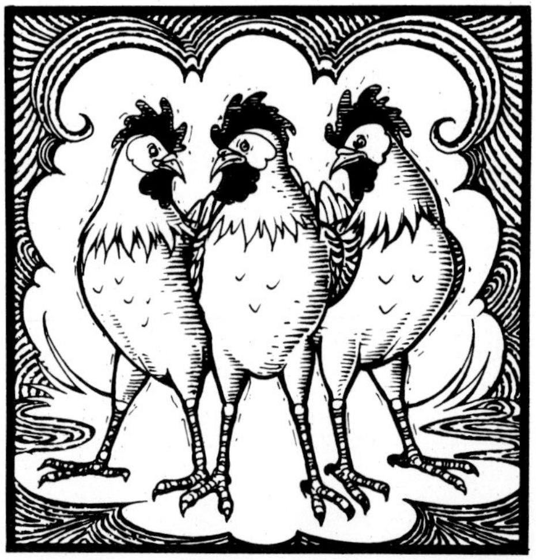

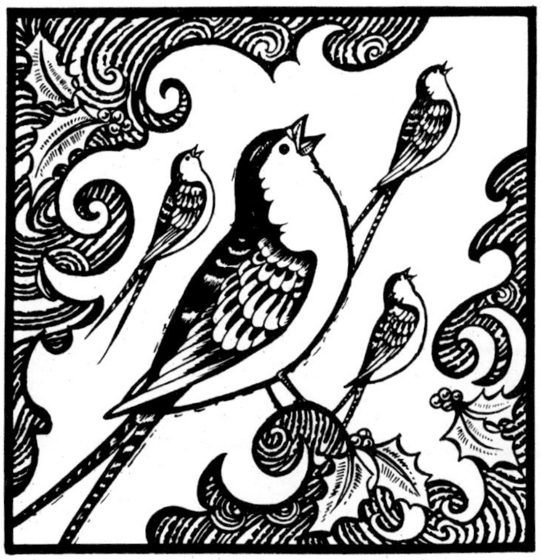
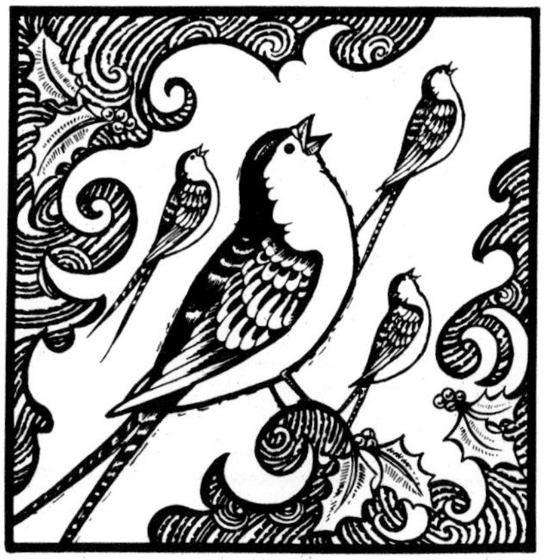
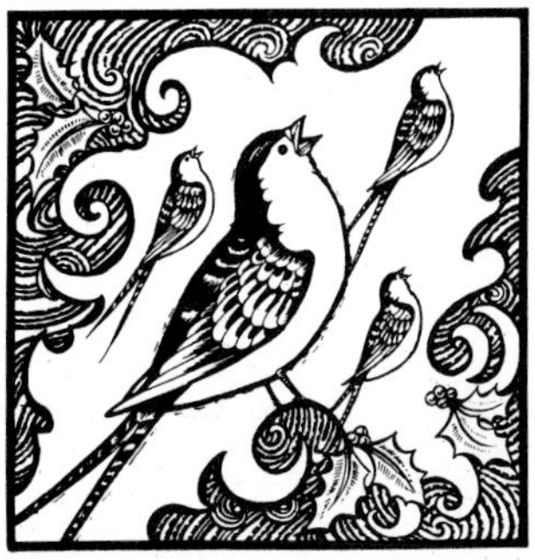
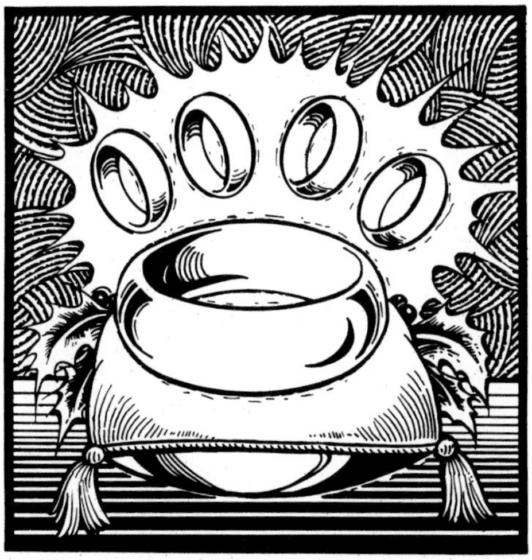
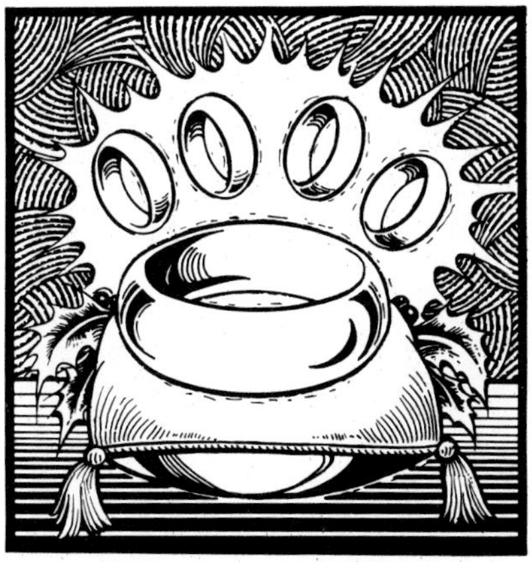
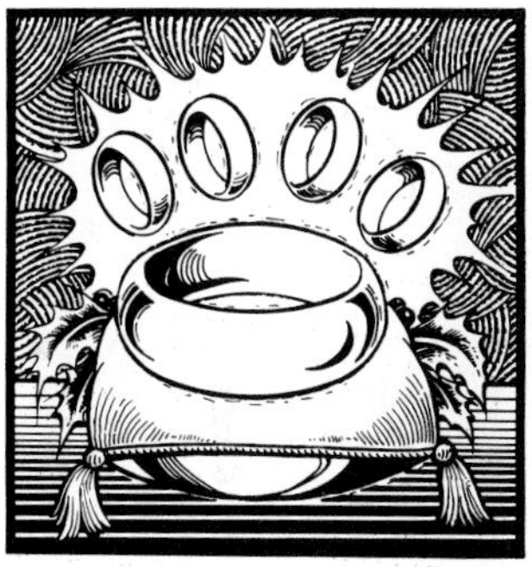
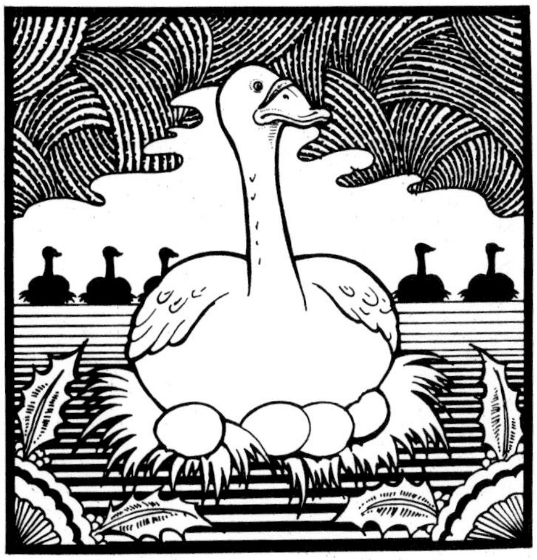
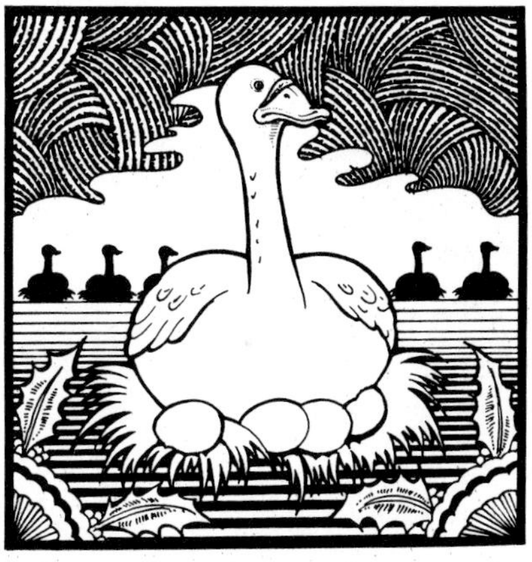
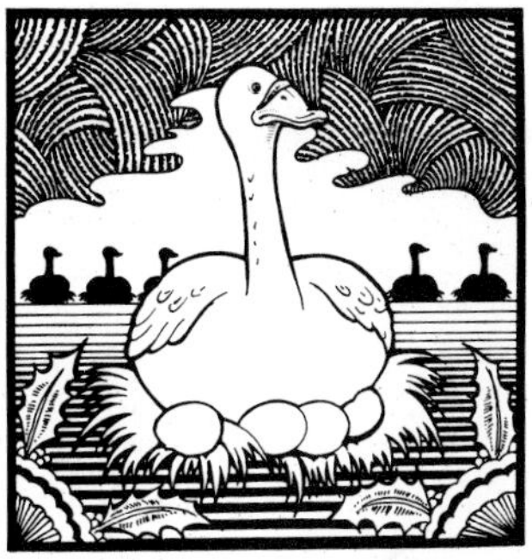

Characters

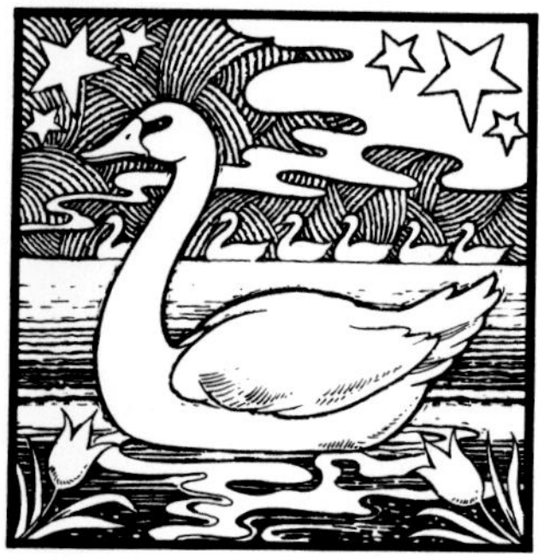
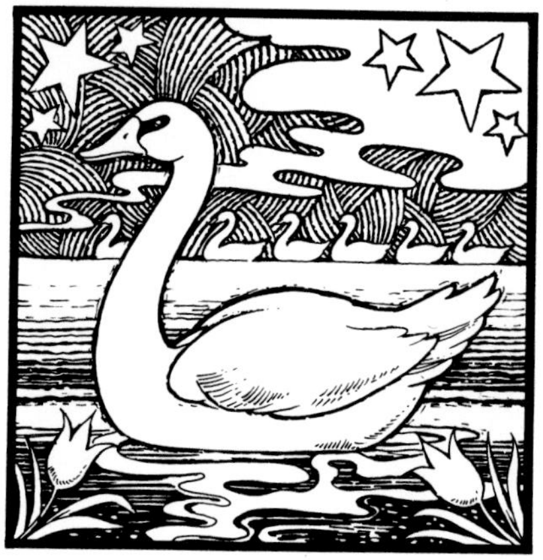
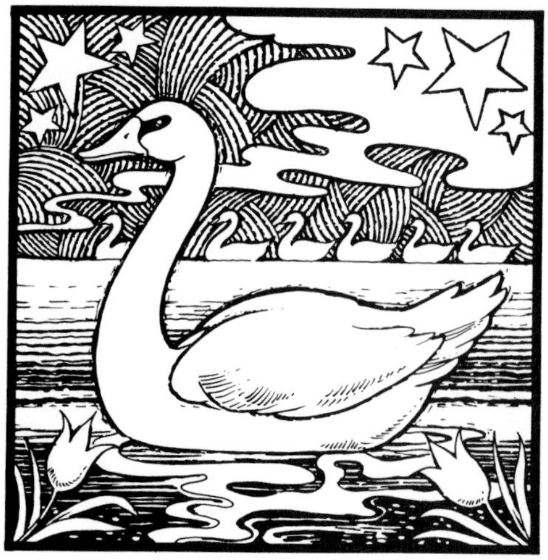
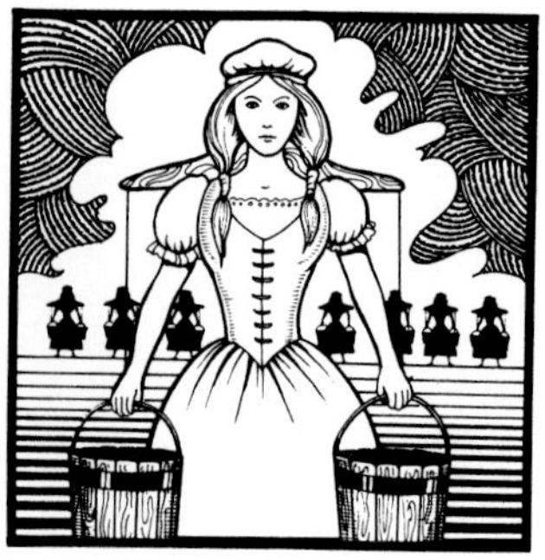
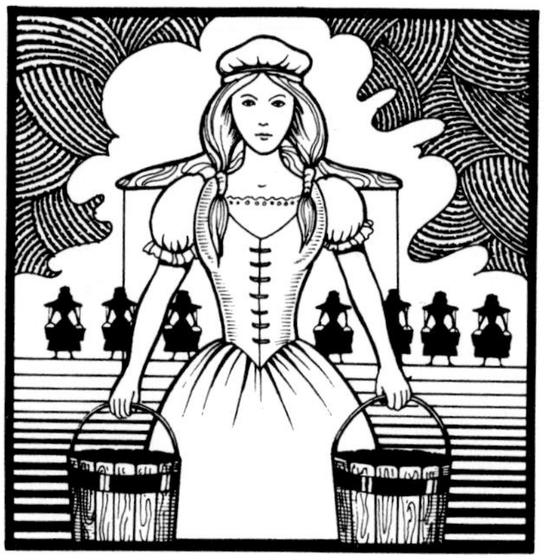
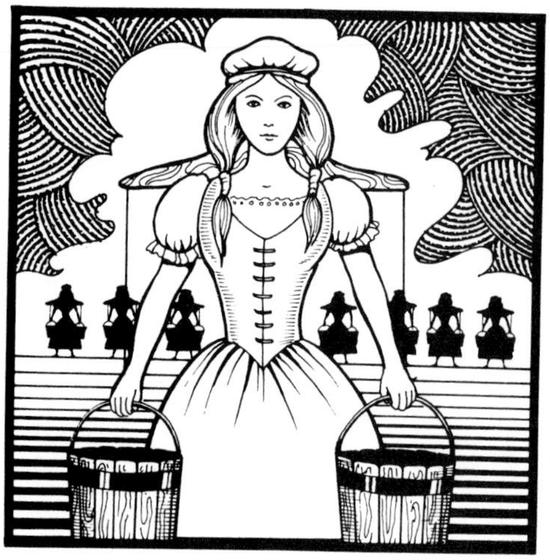
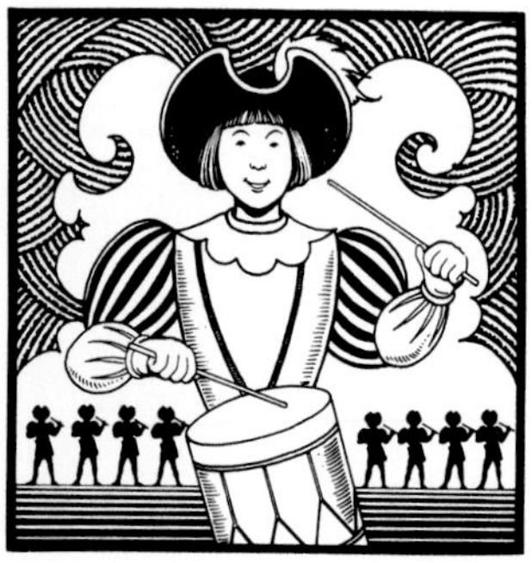
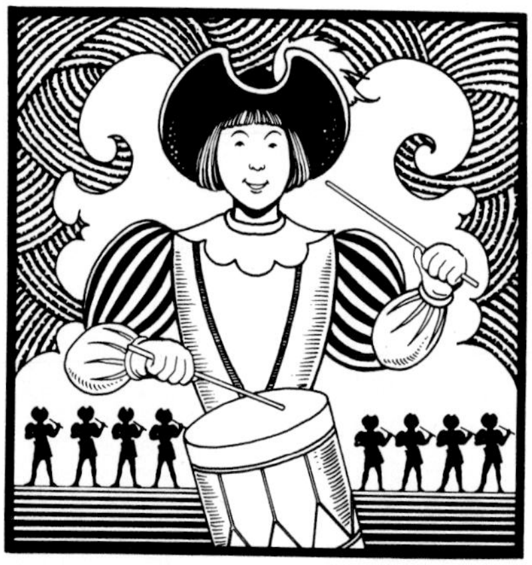
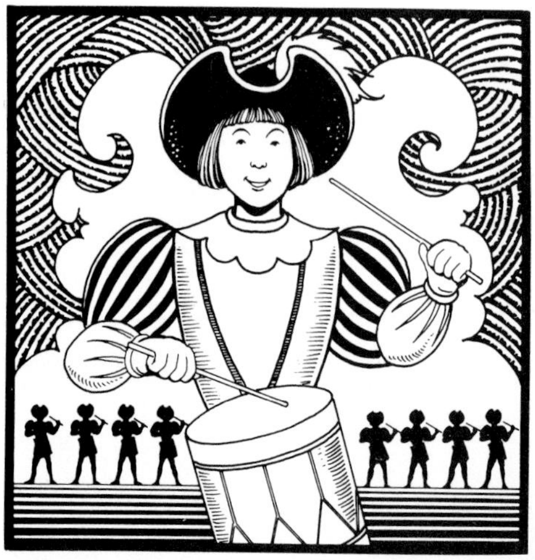

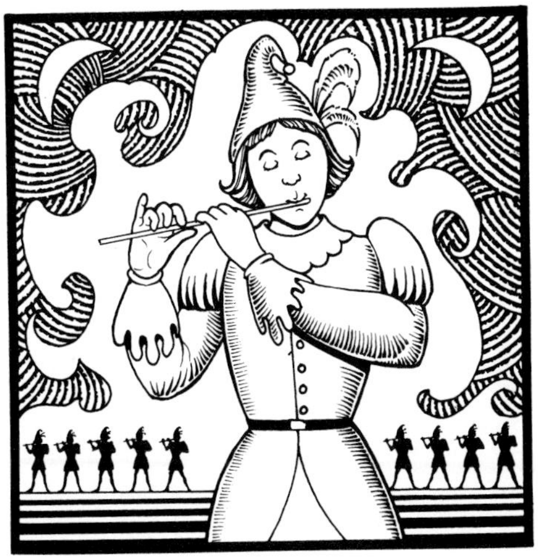

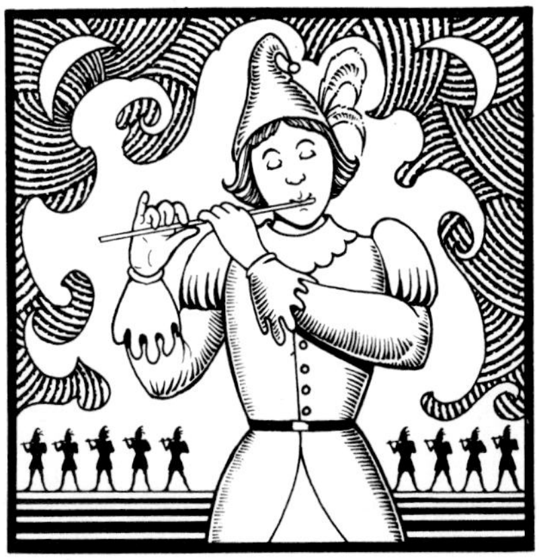

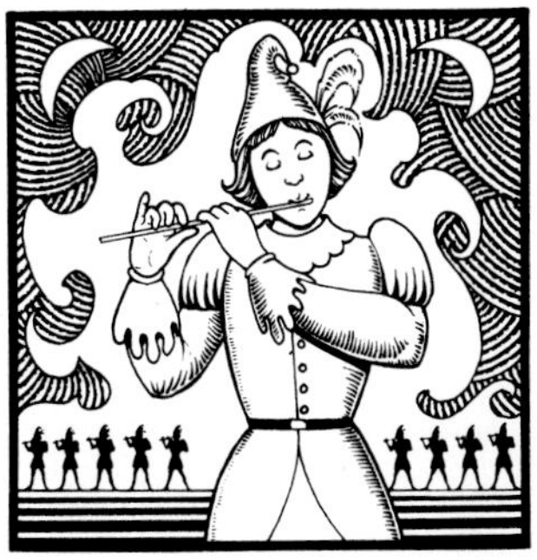

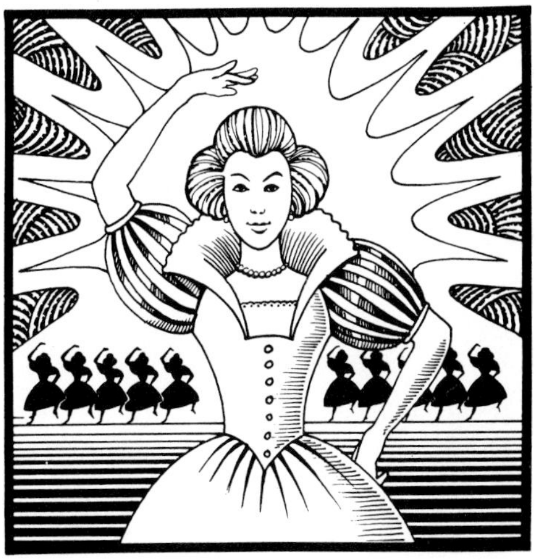

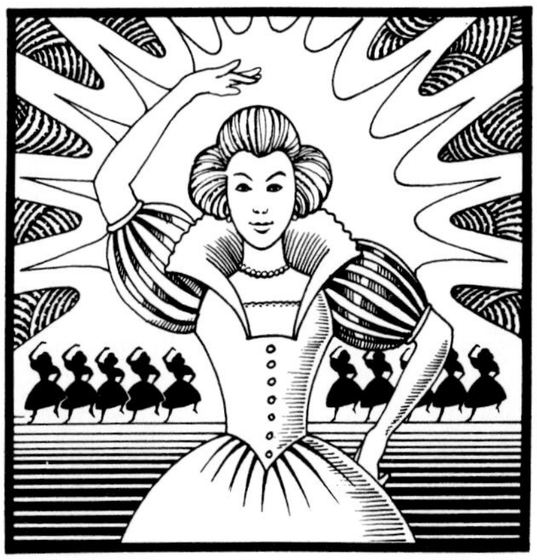

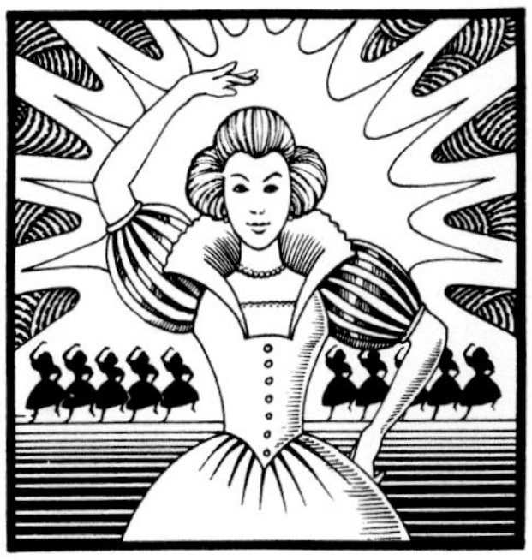

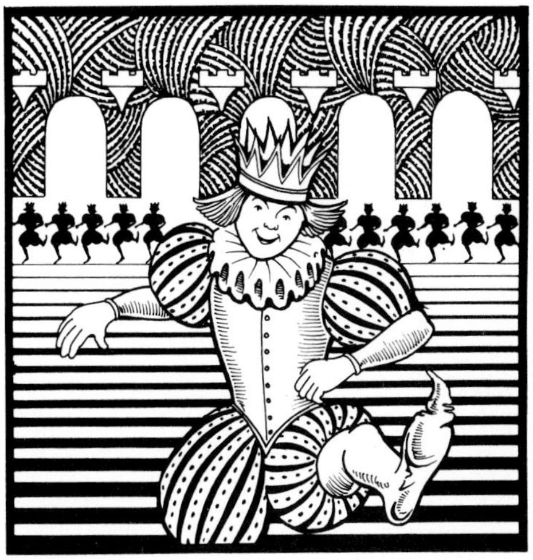

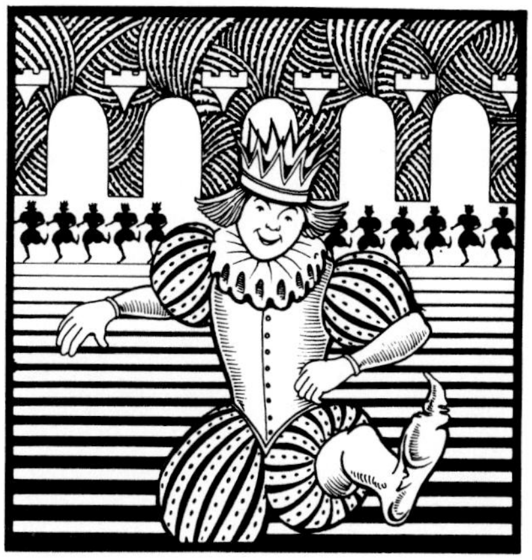

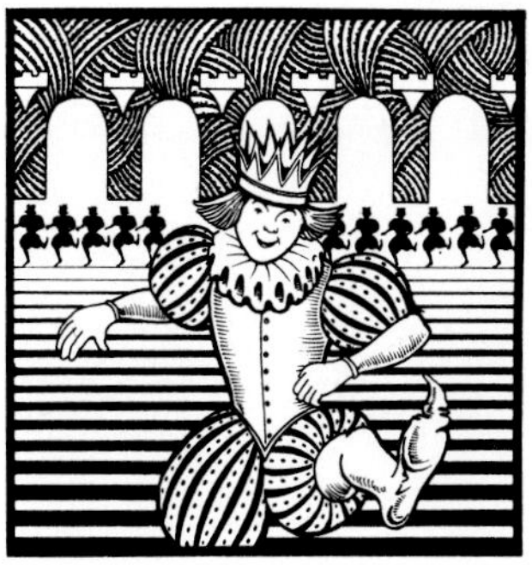

■ Characters

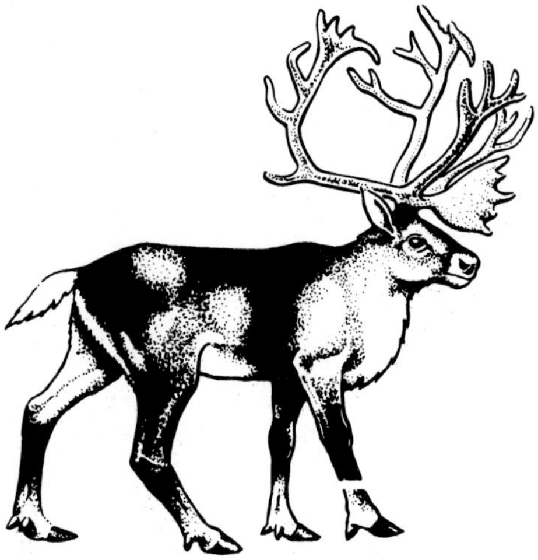

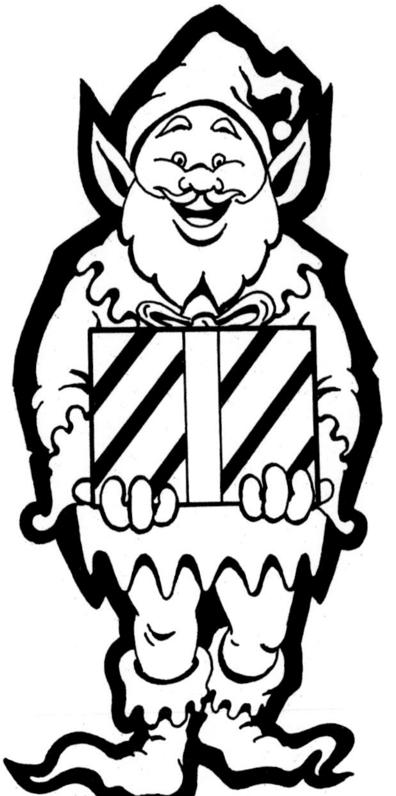

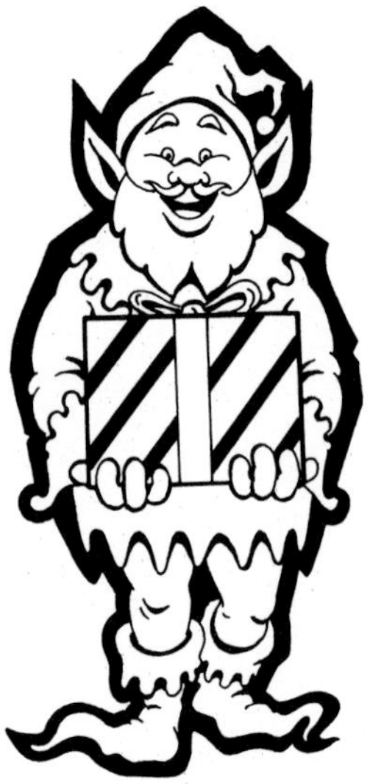

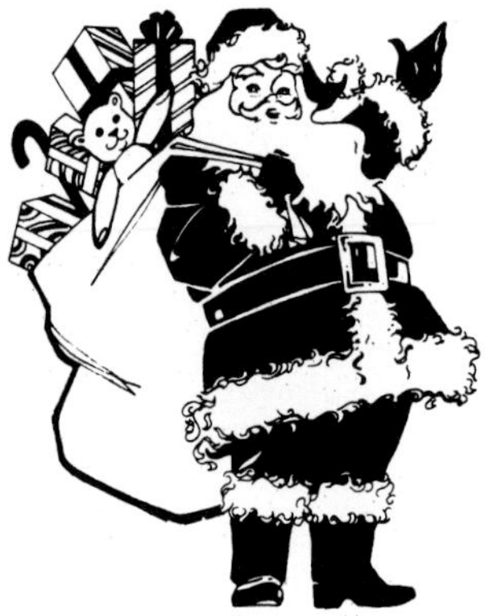

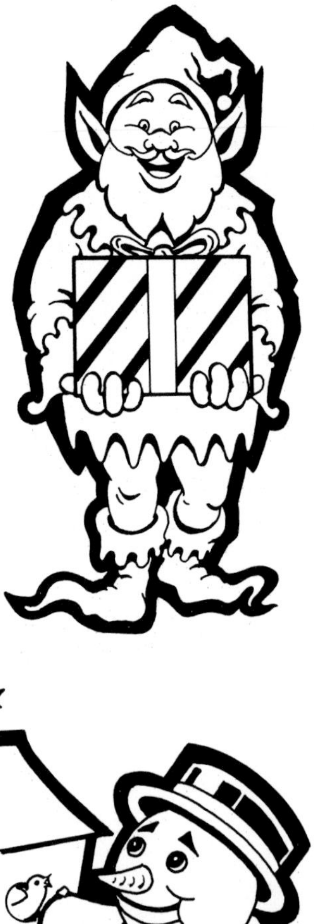

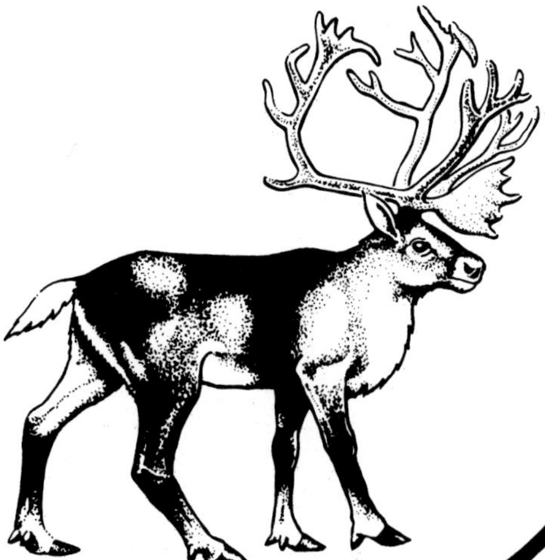

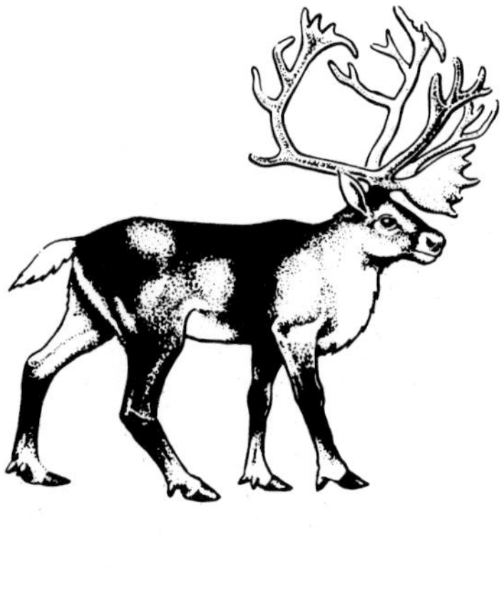

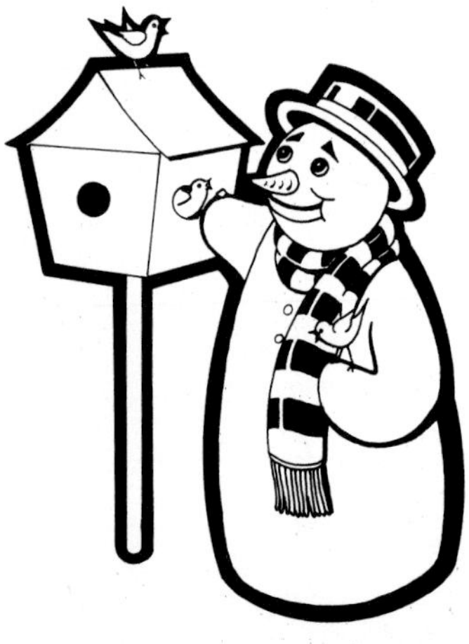

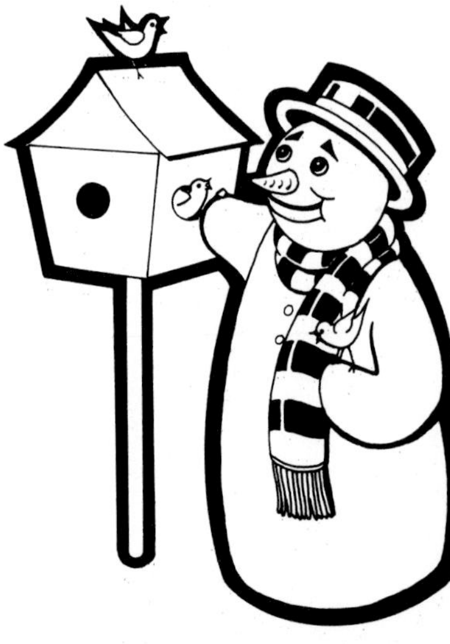

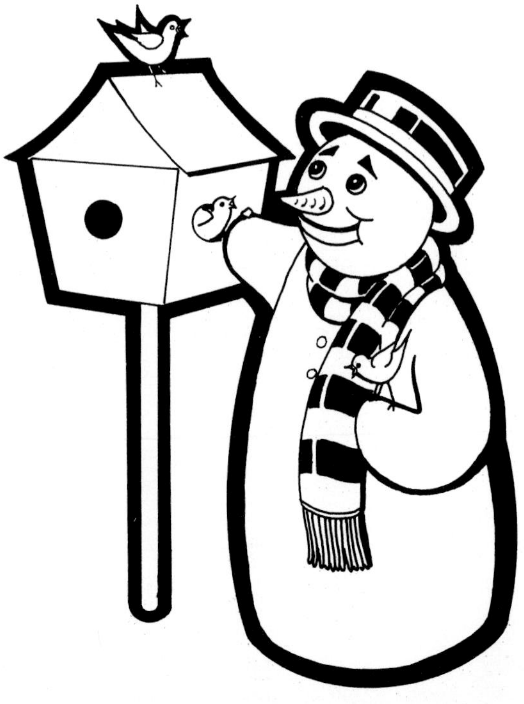

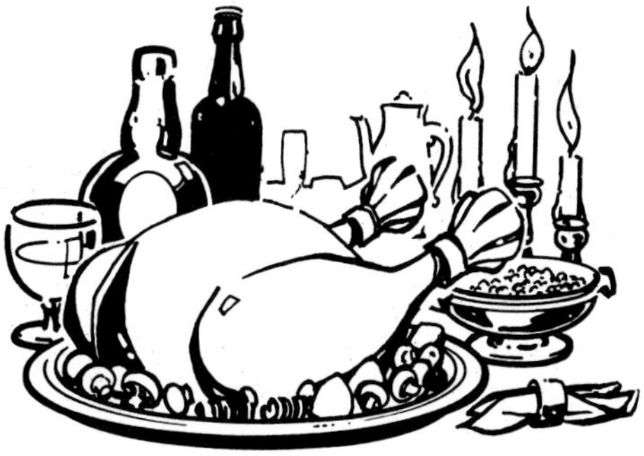

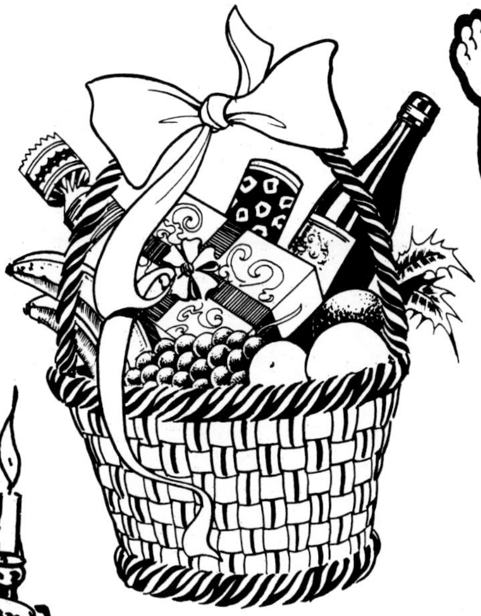

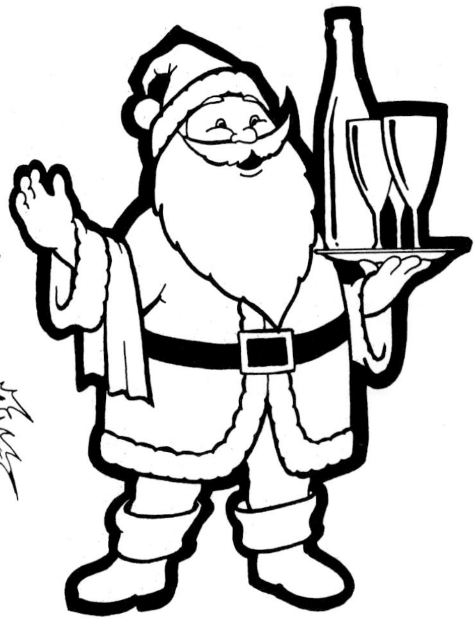

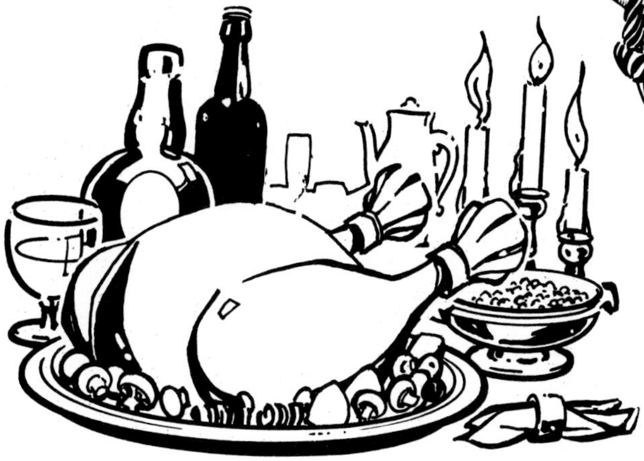

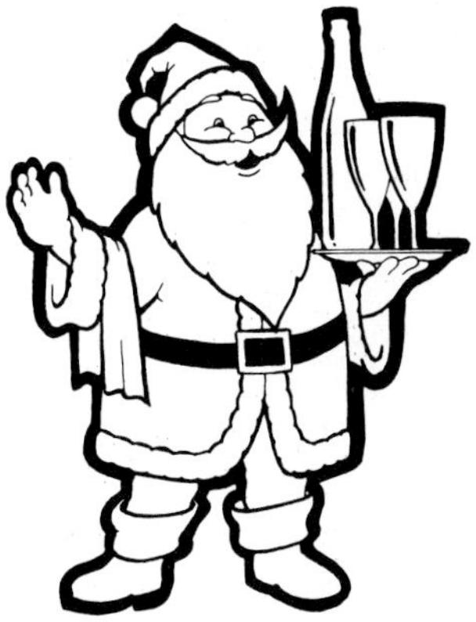

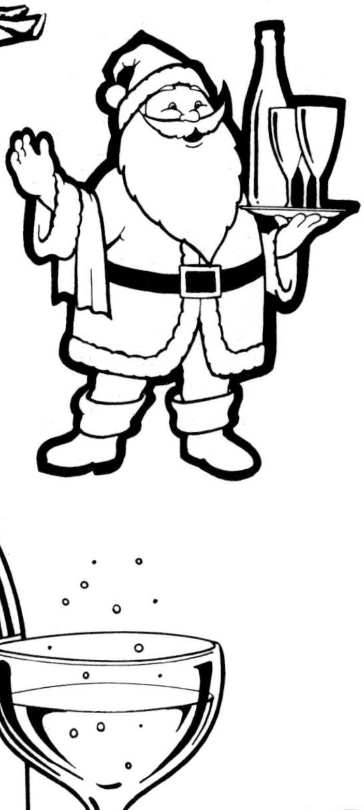

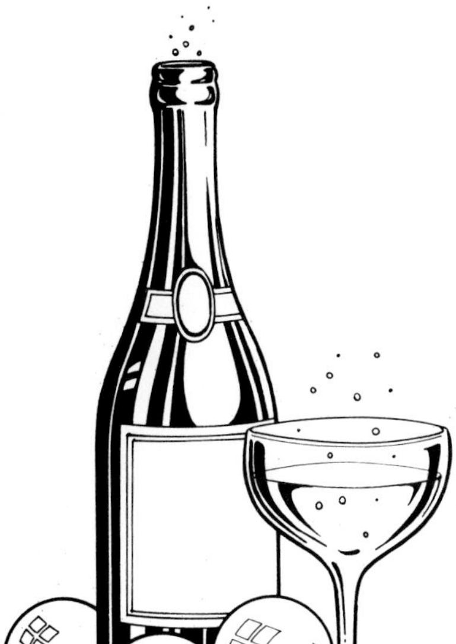

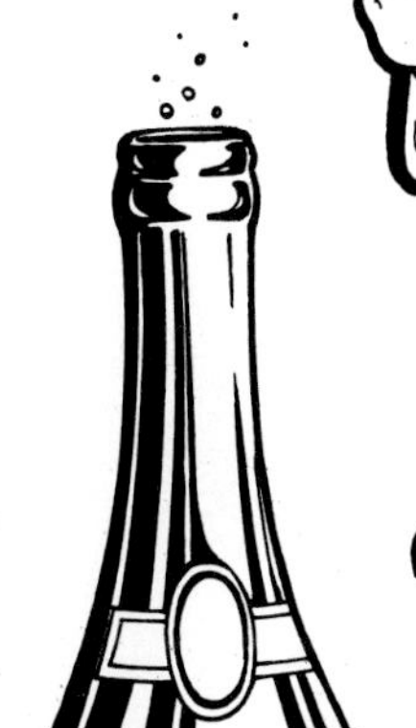
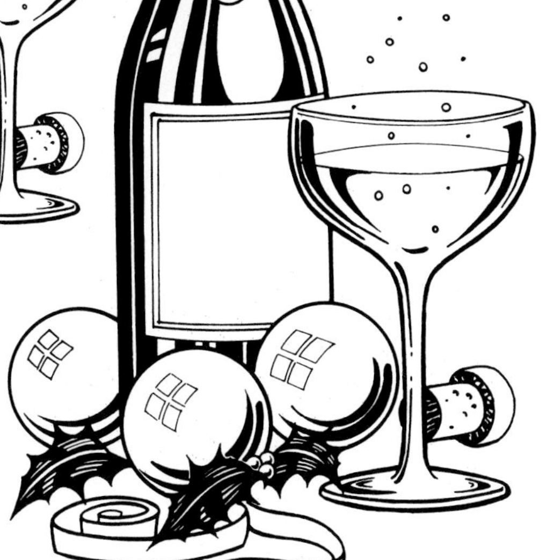

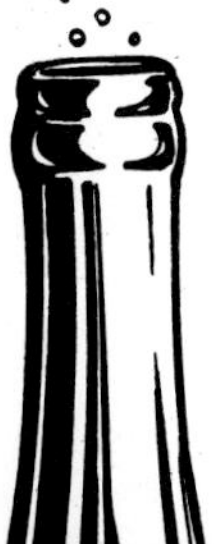
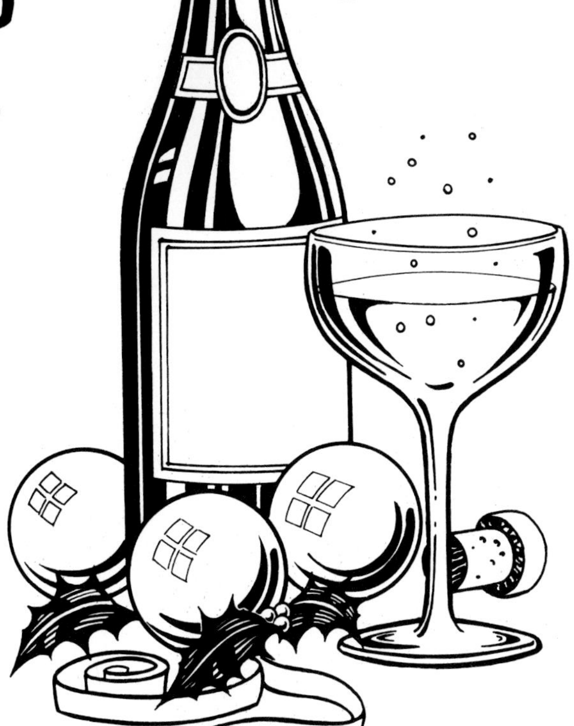

■ Decorations

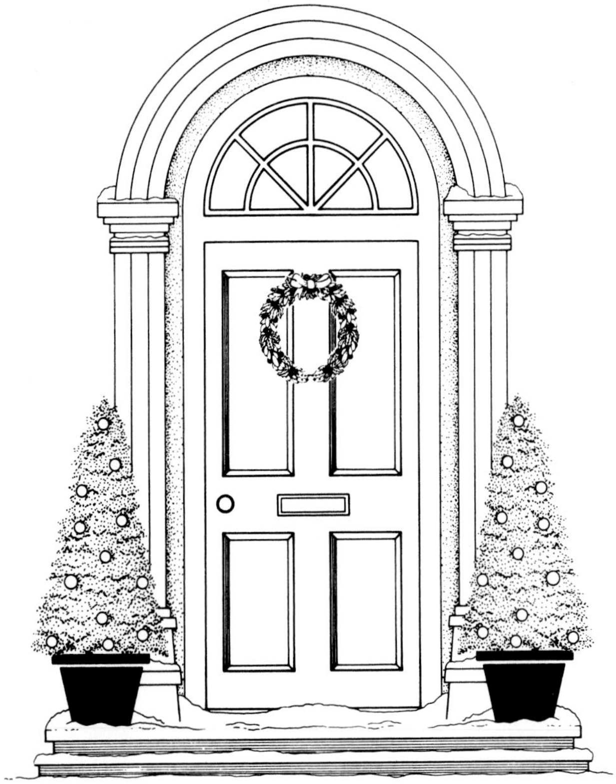

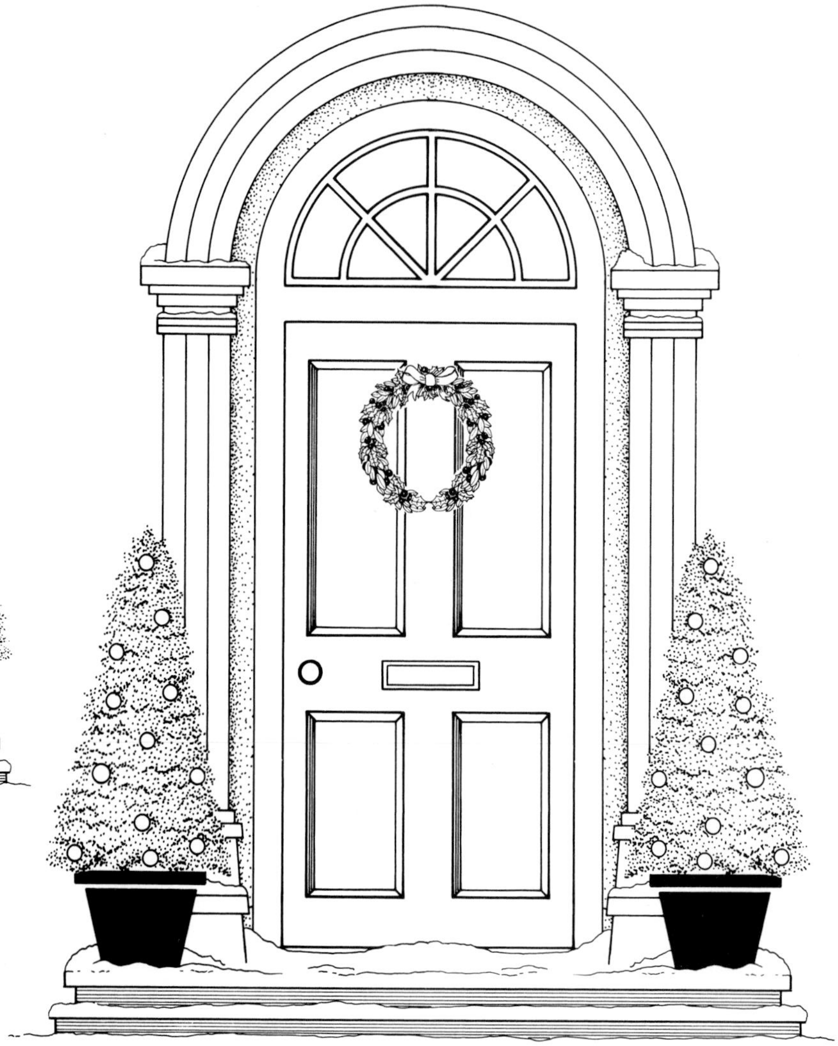

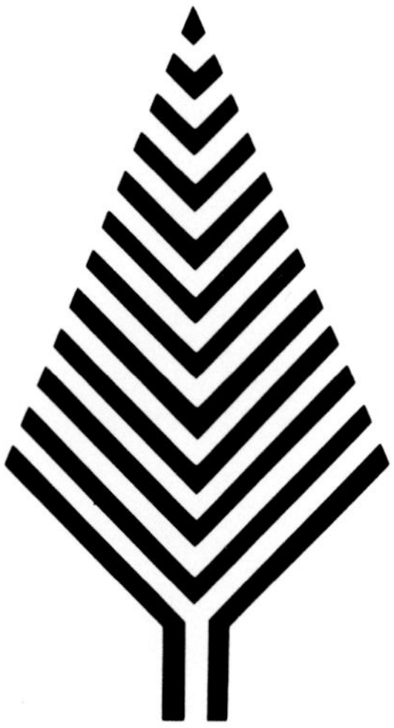

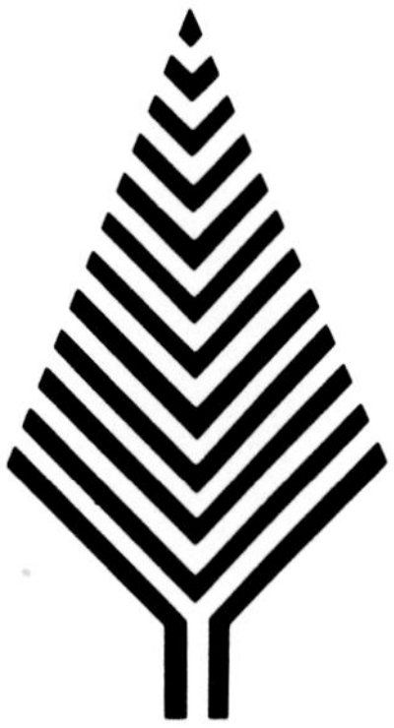

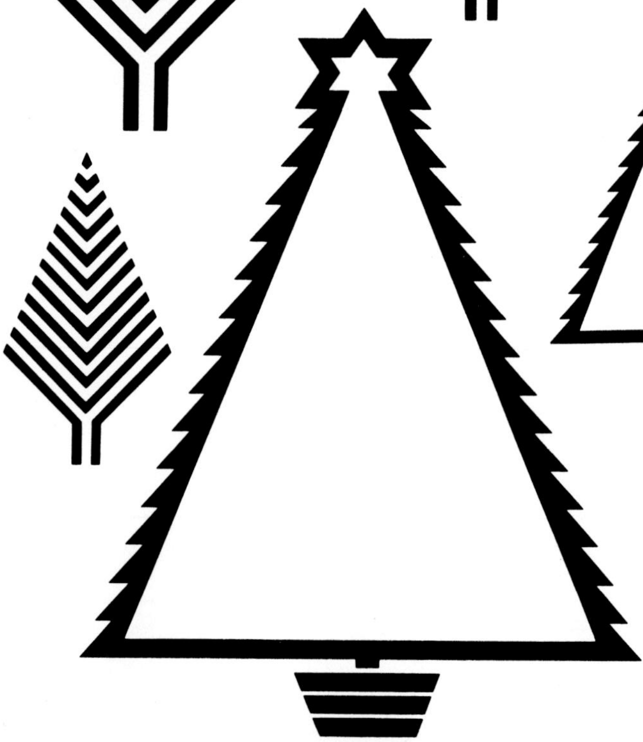

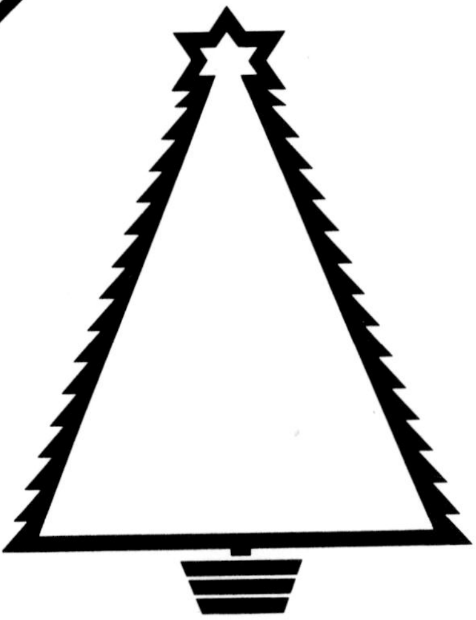

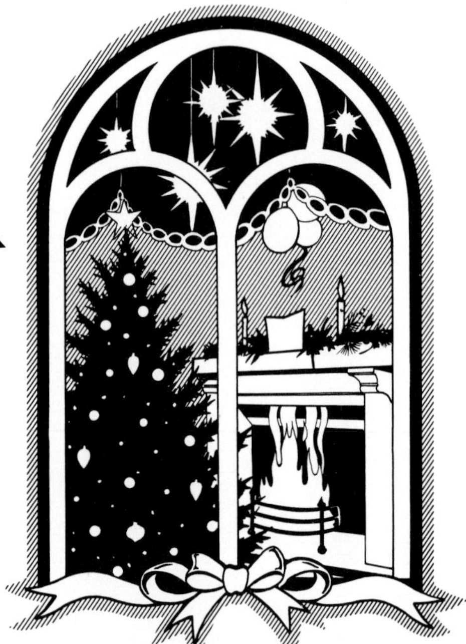

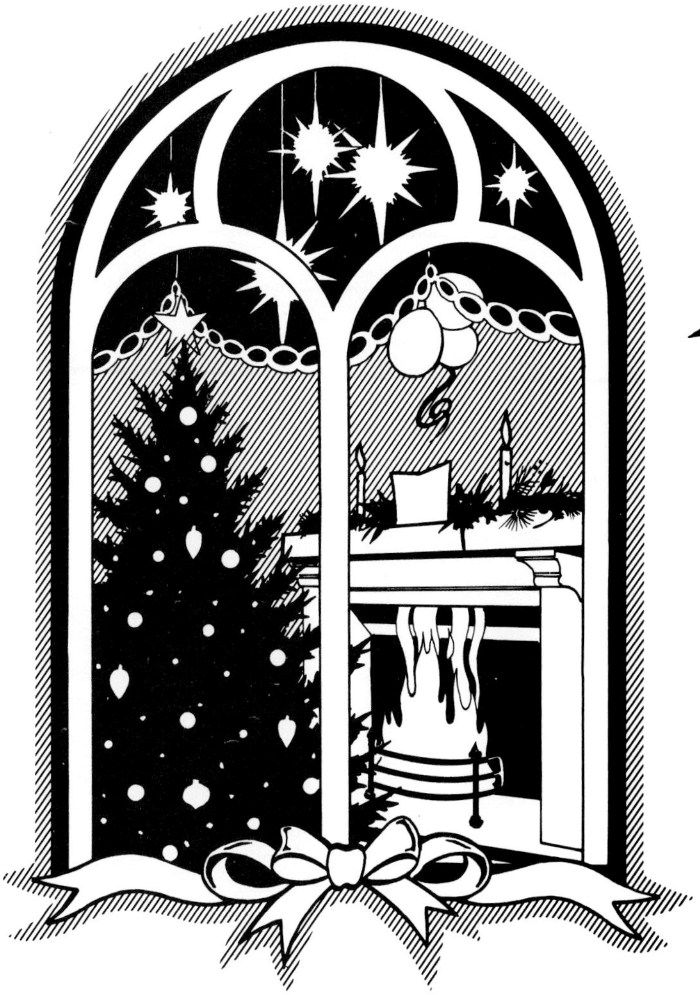

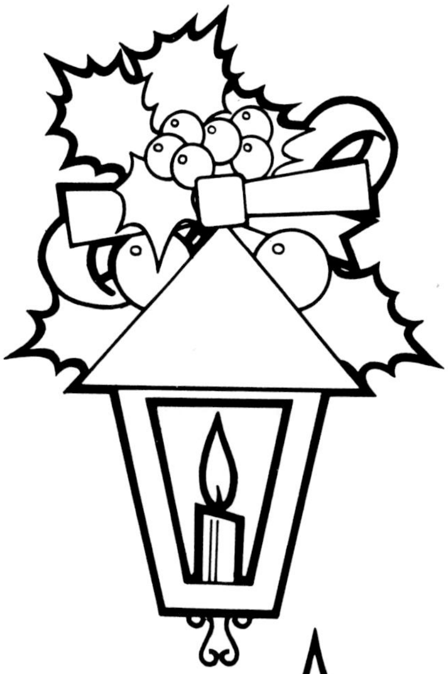

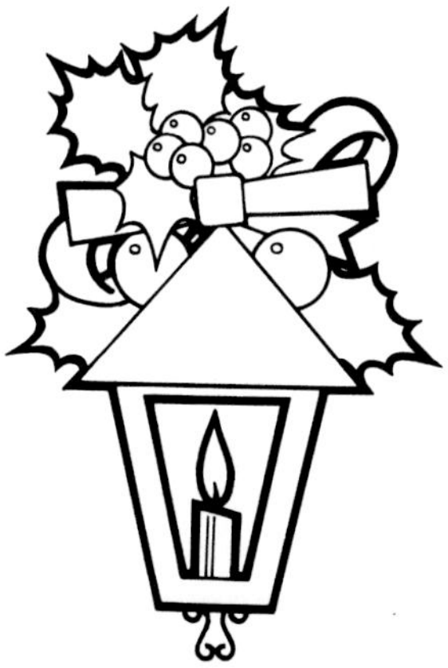

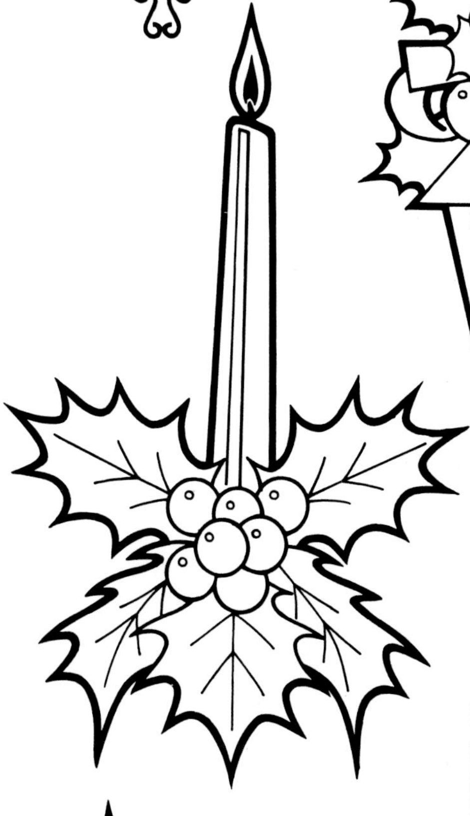

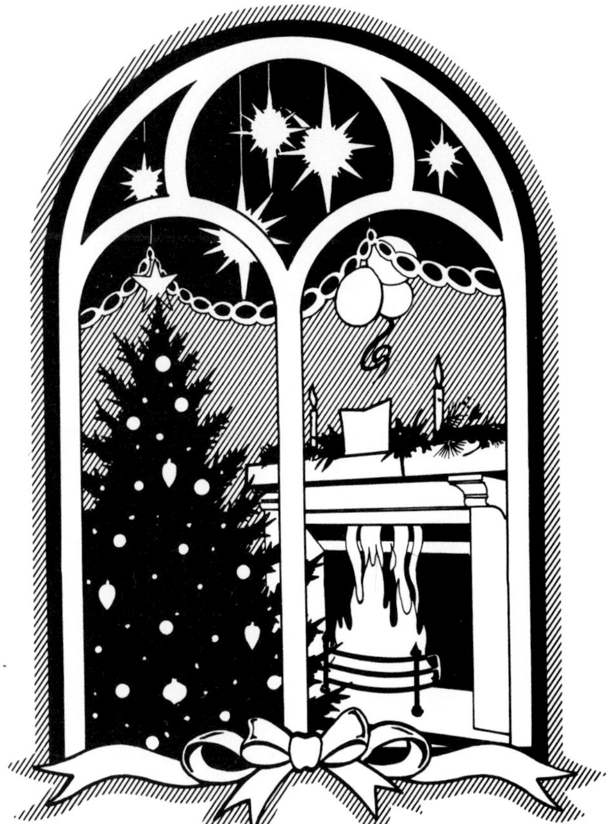

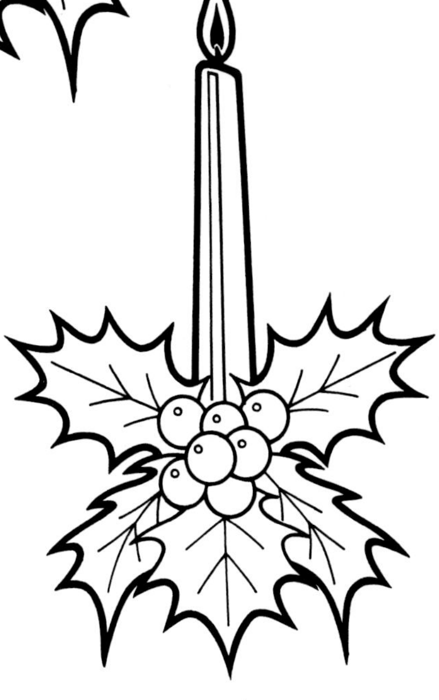

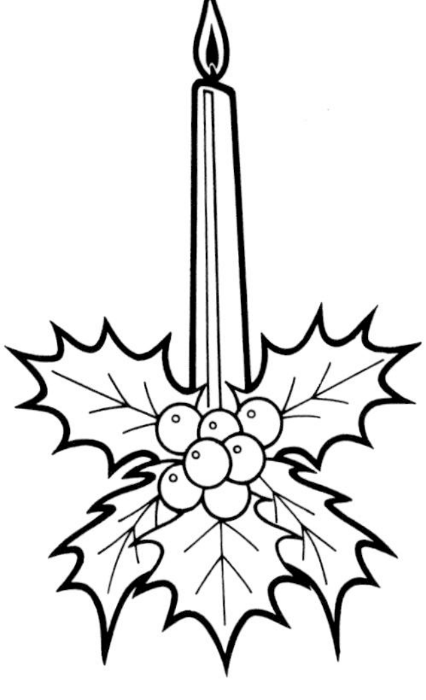

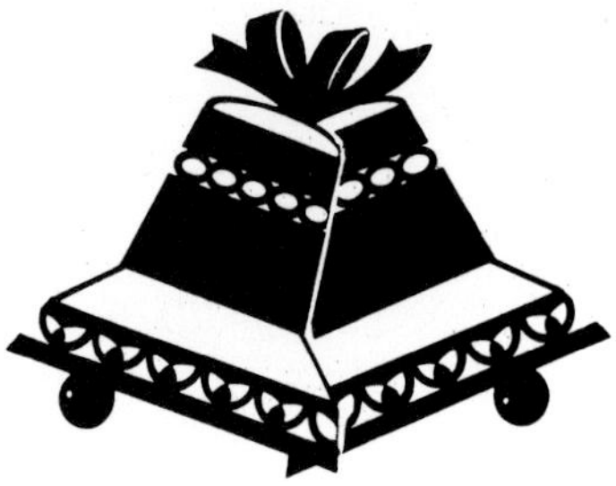

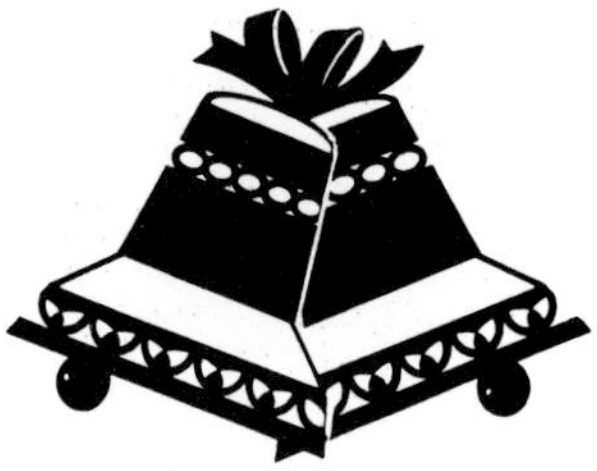

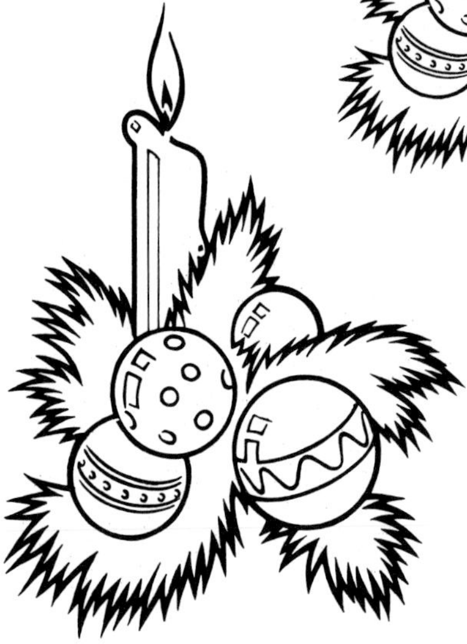

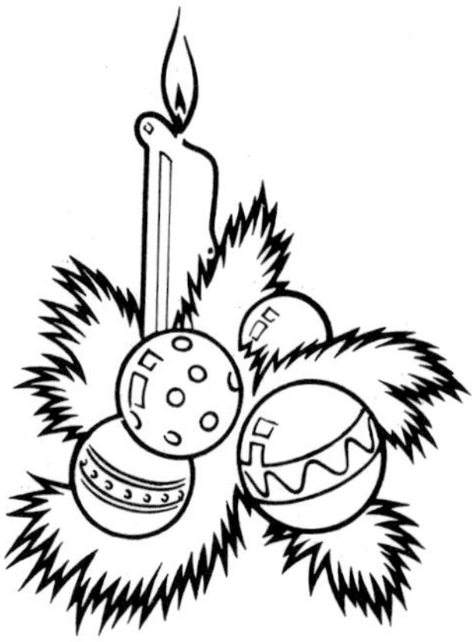

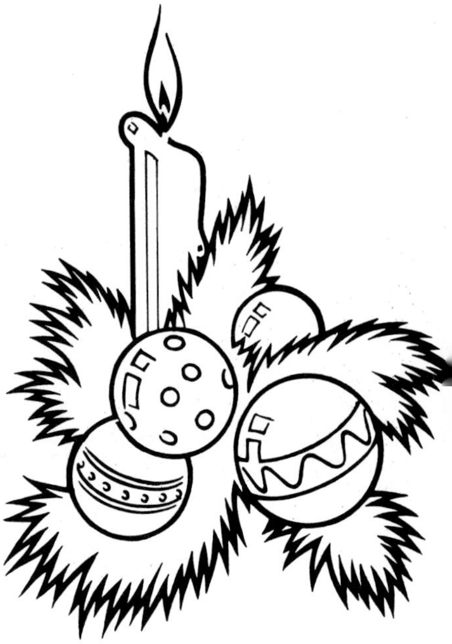

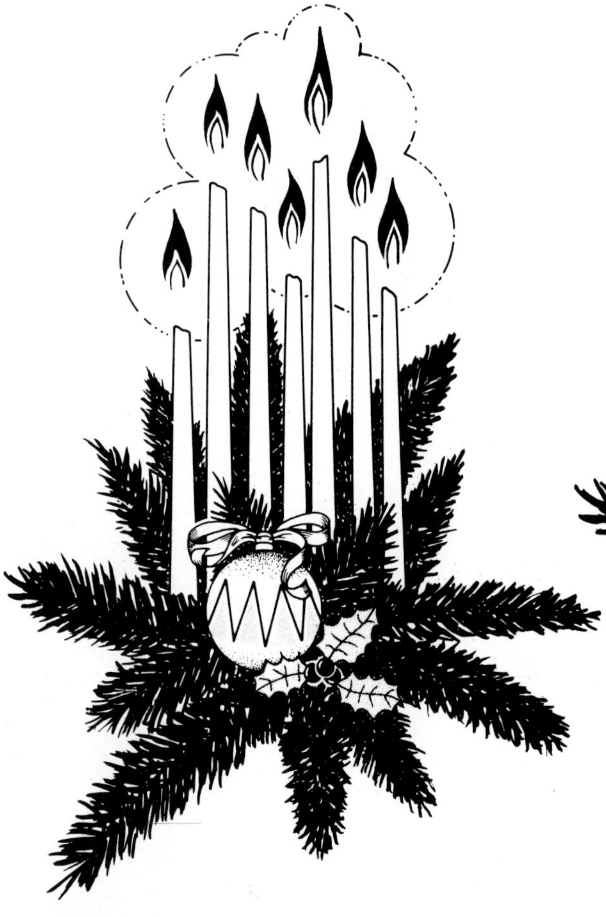

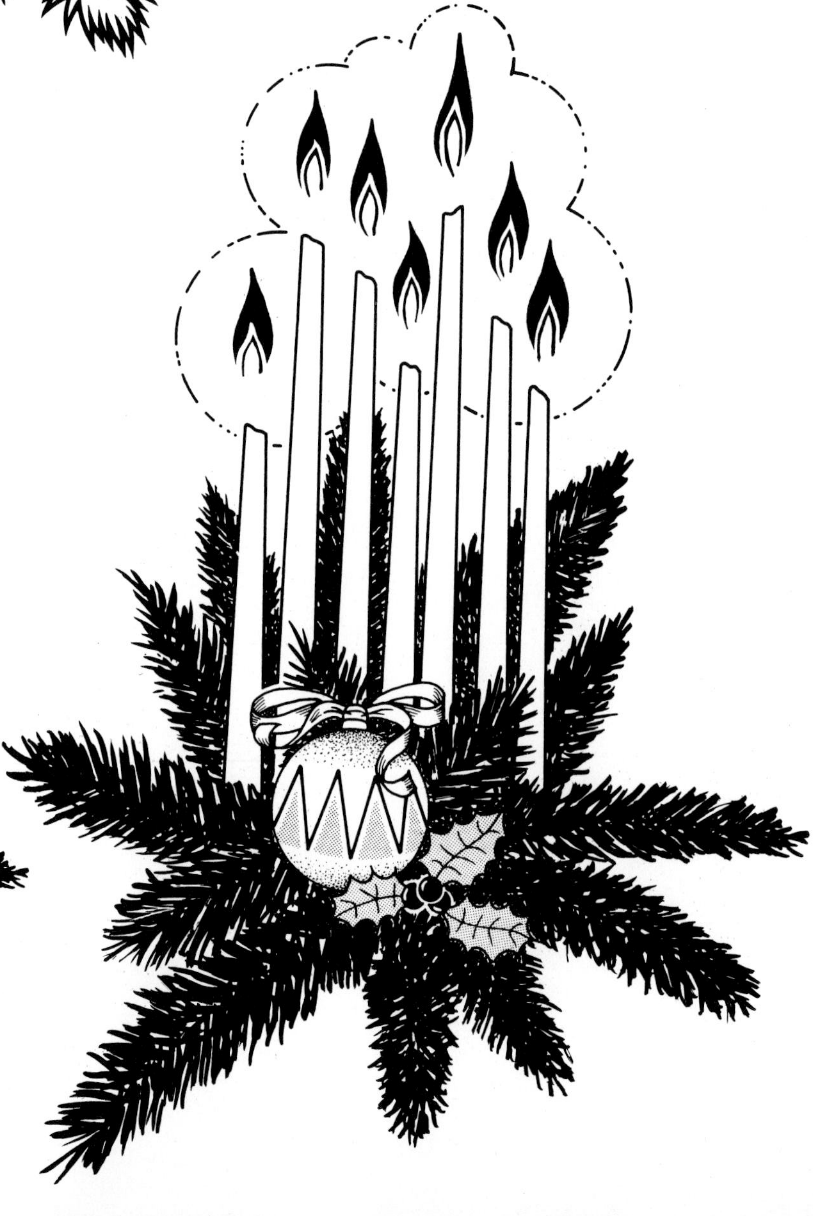

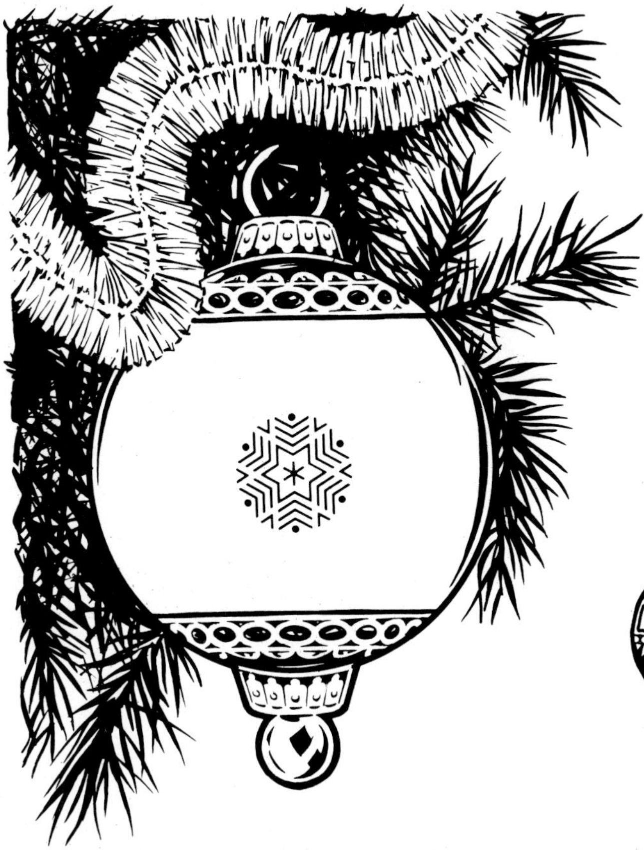

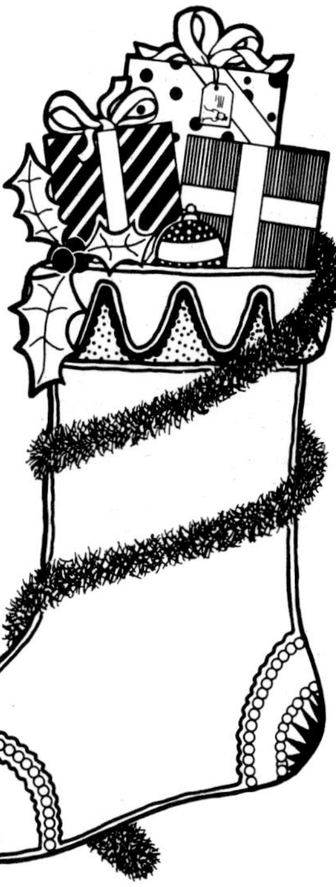

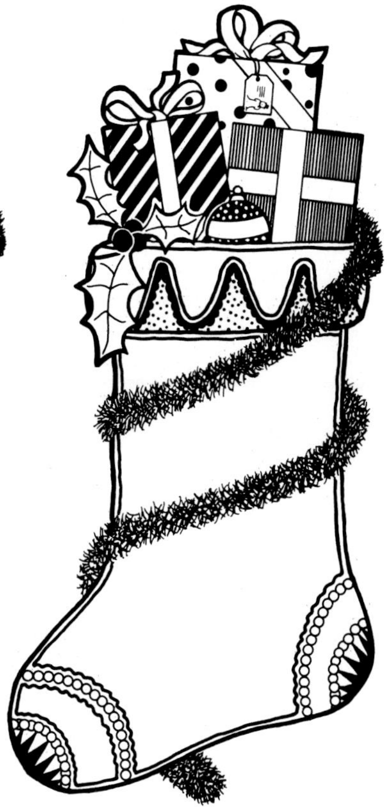

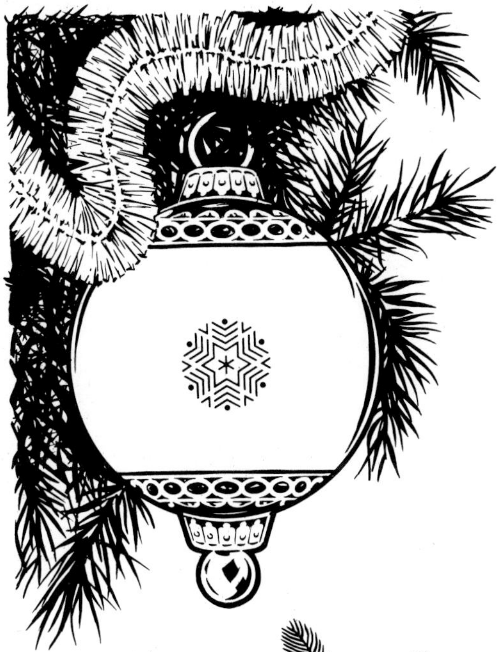

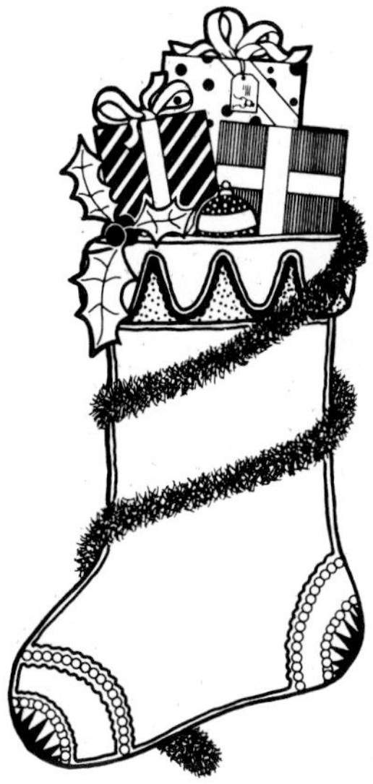

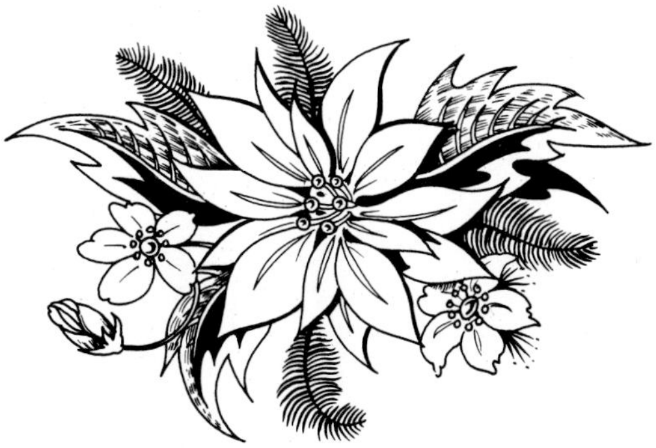

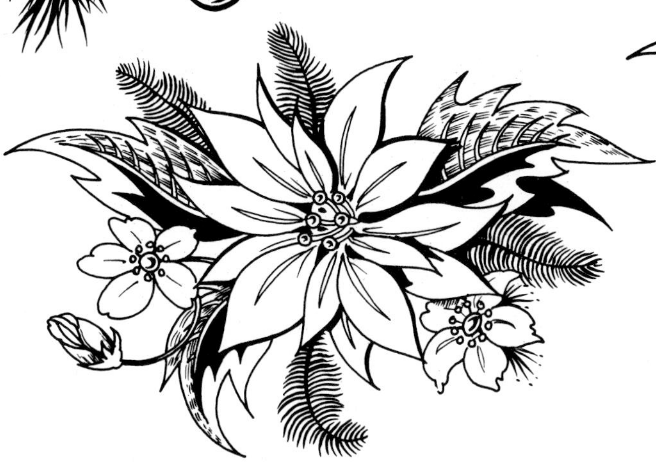

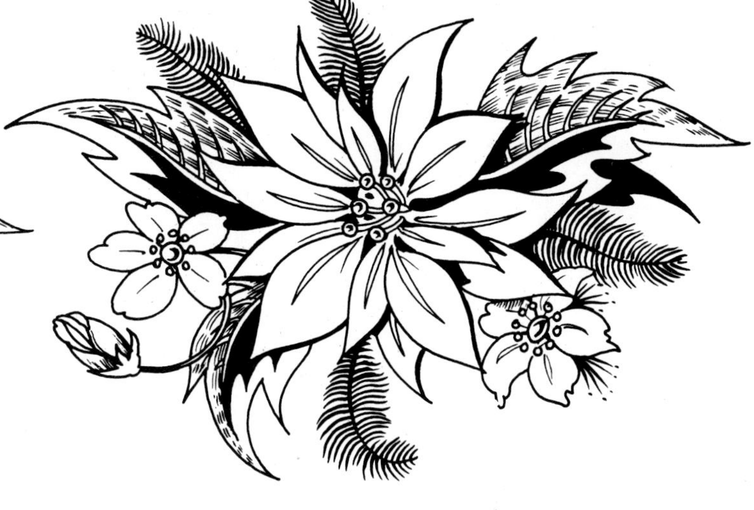

■ Decorations

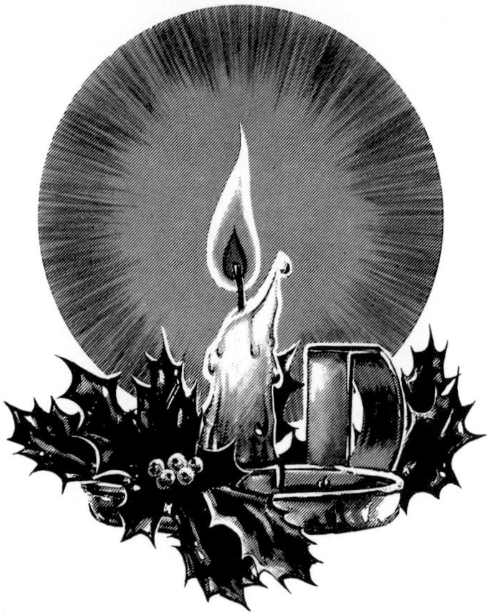

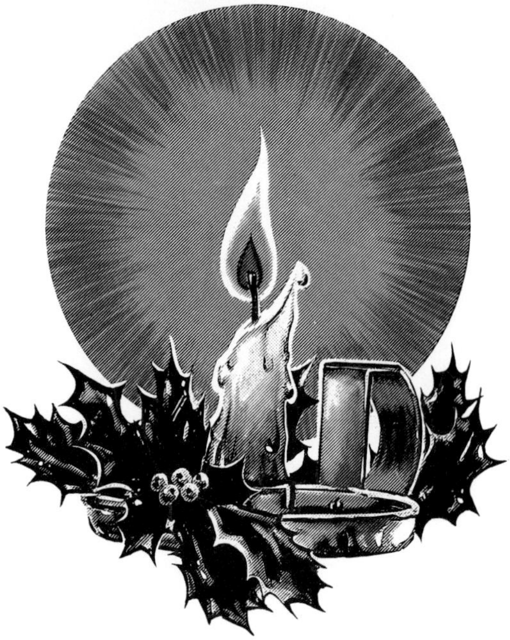

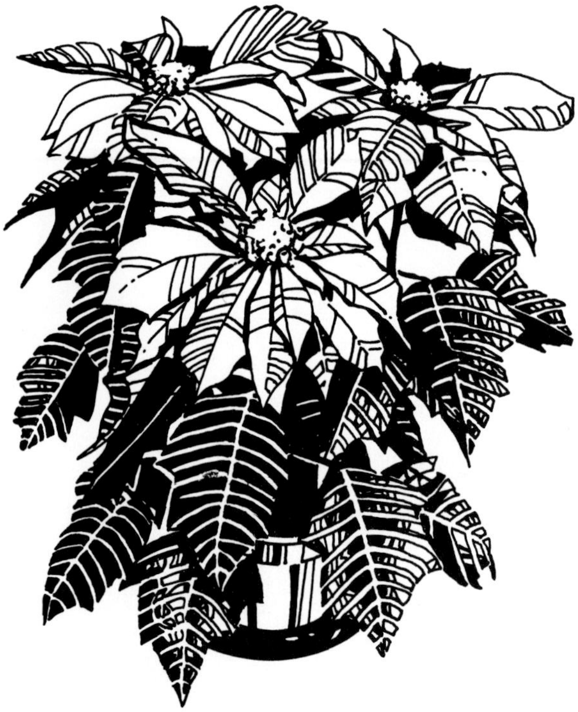

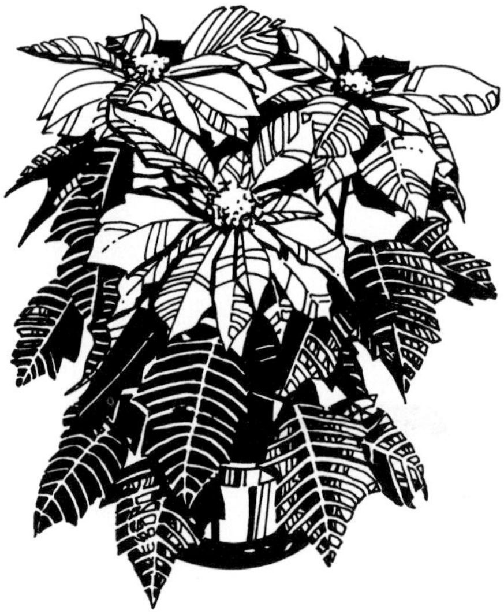

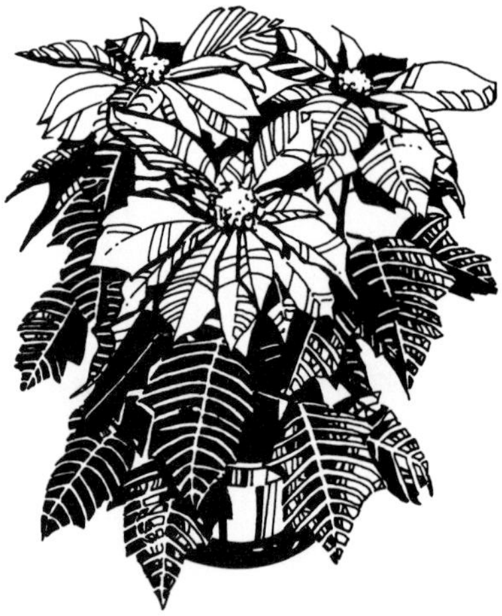

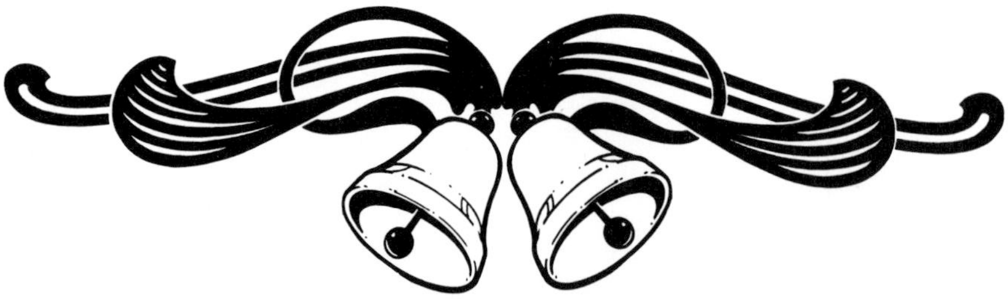

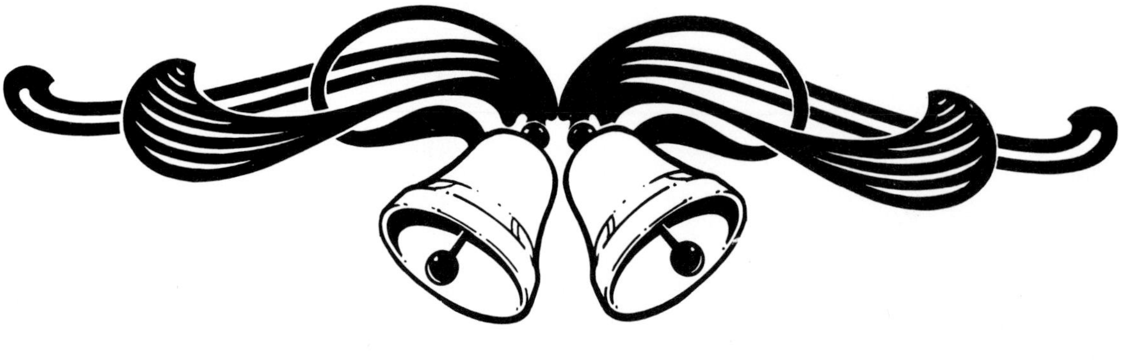

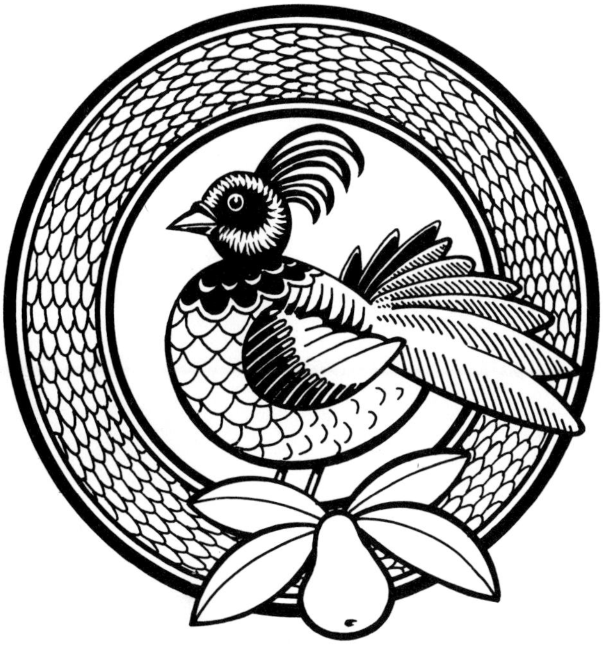

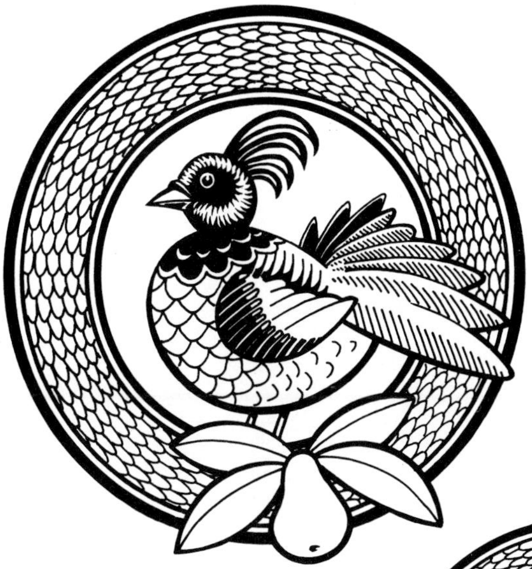

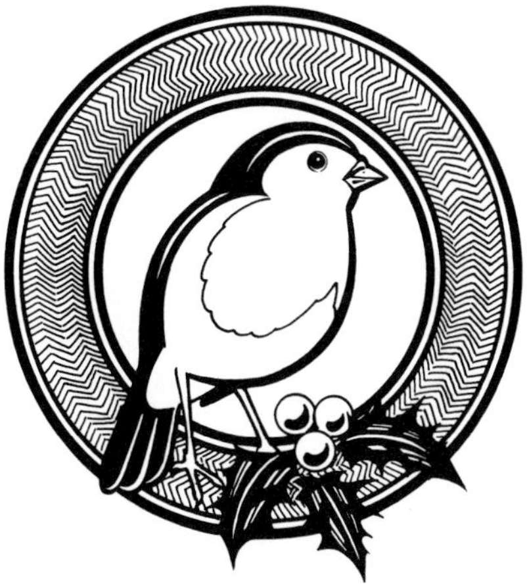

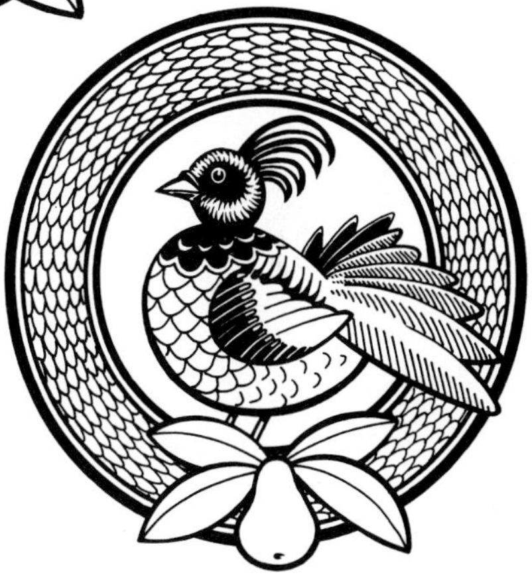

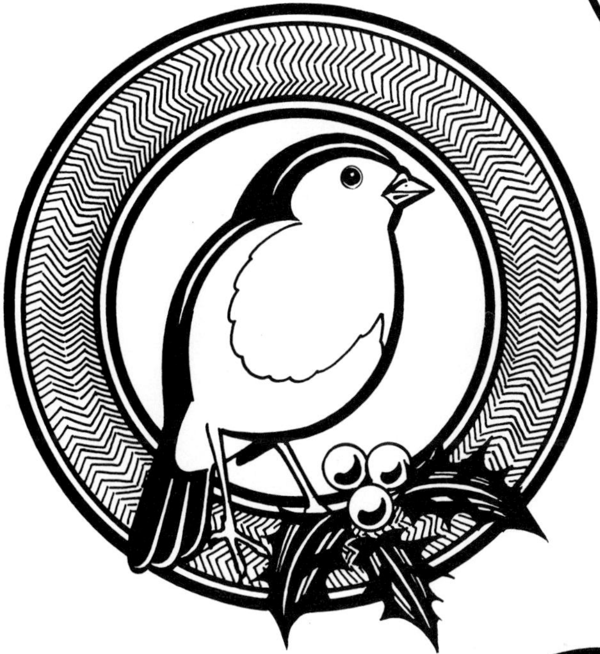

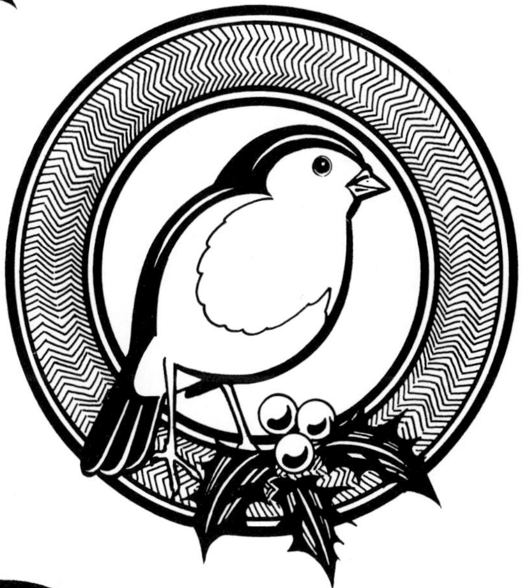

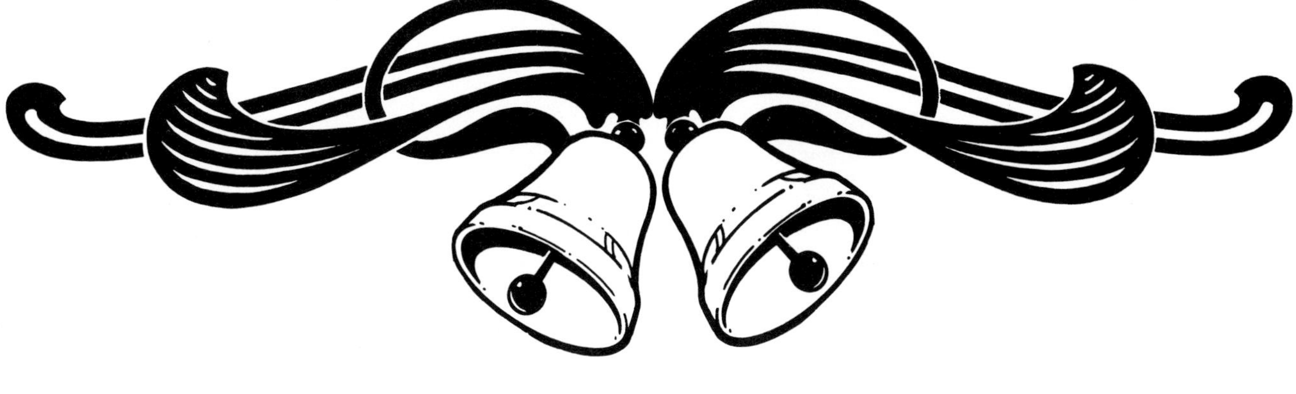

■ Family

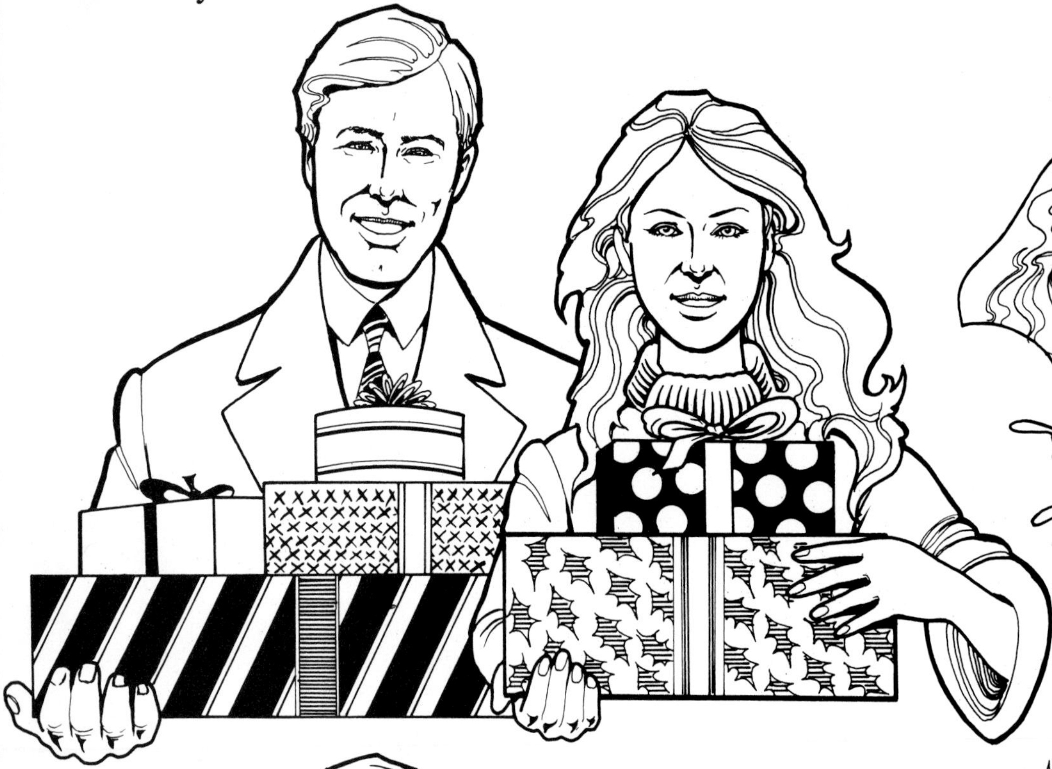

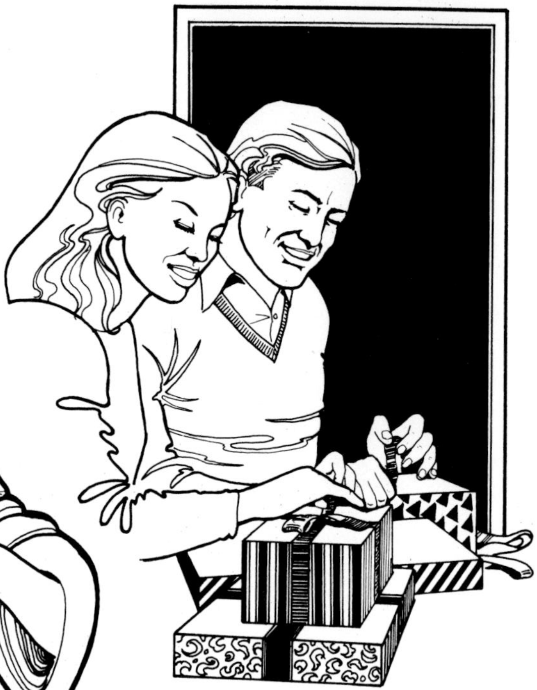

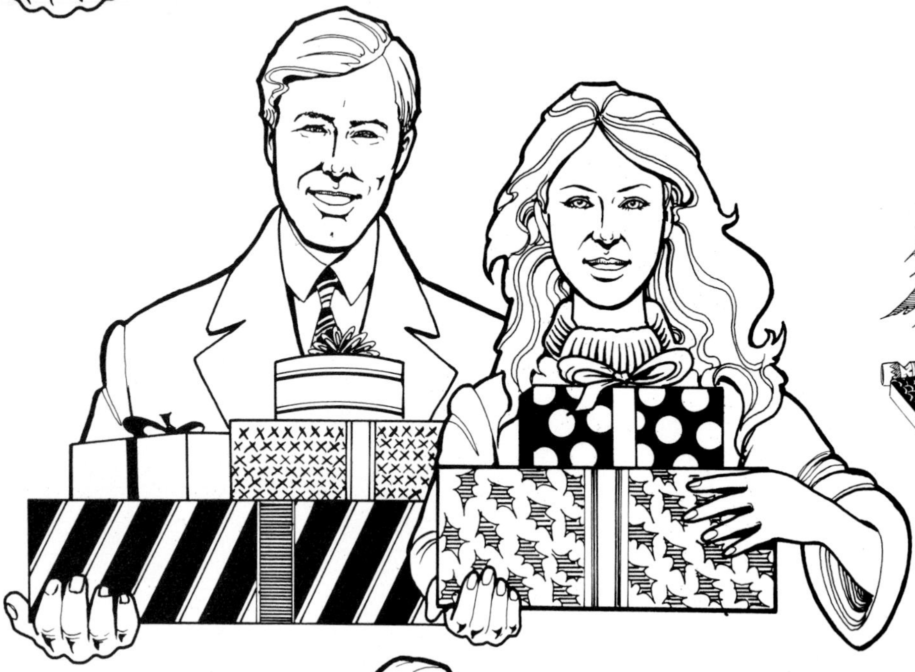

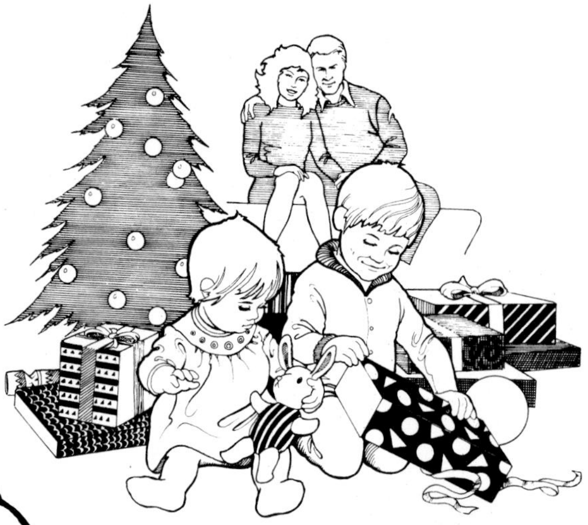

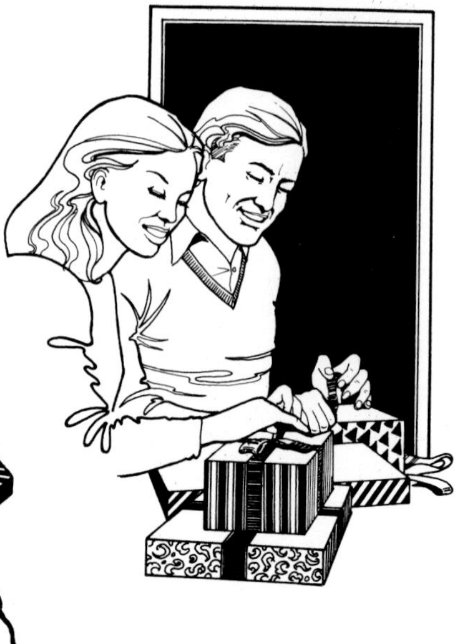

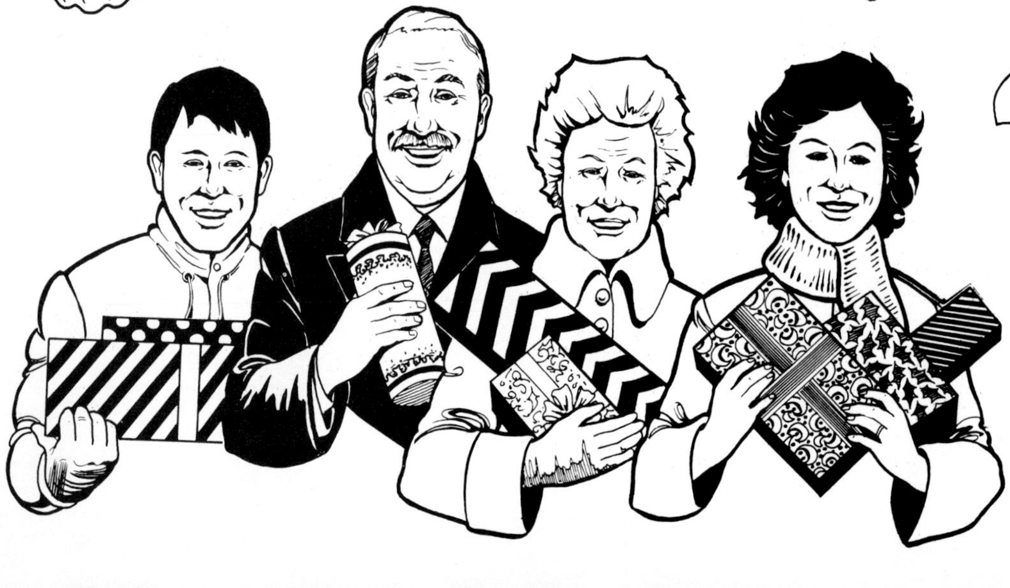

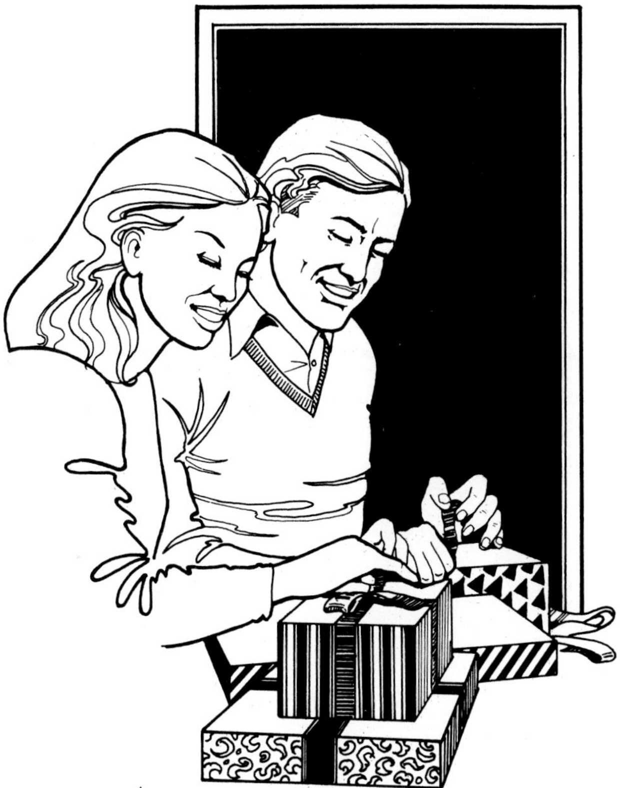

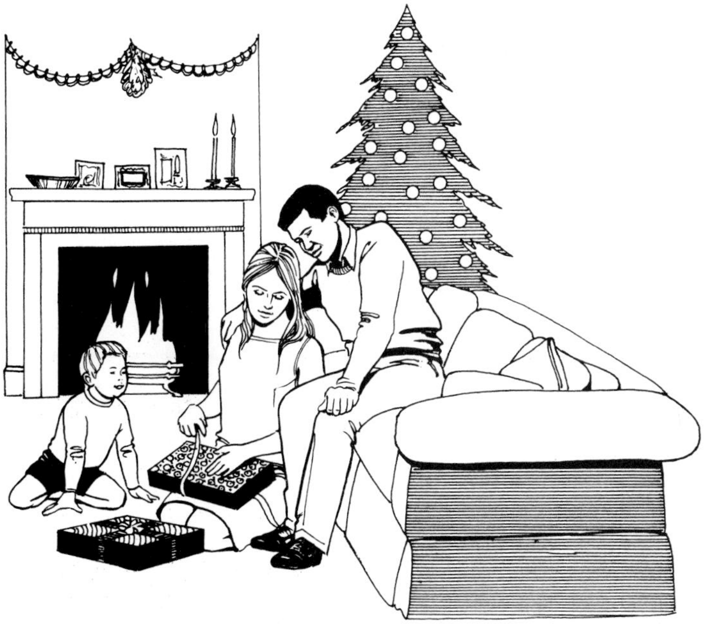

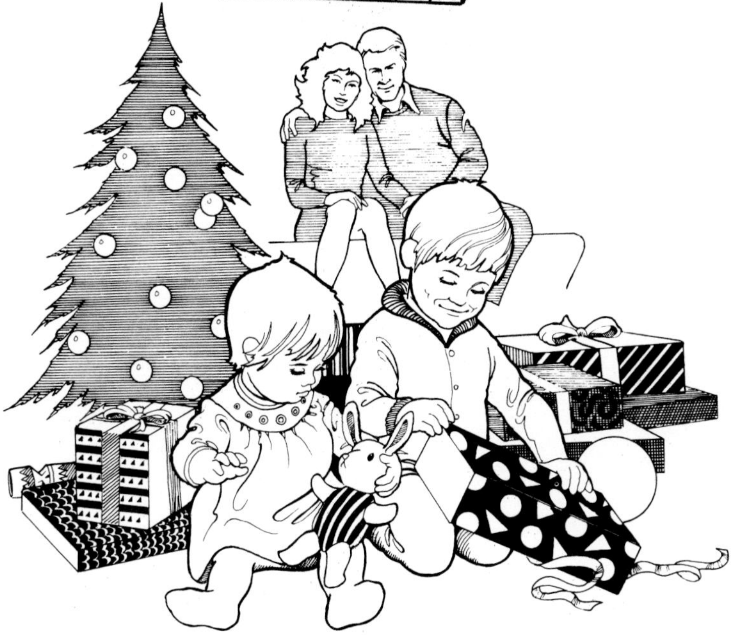

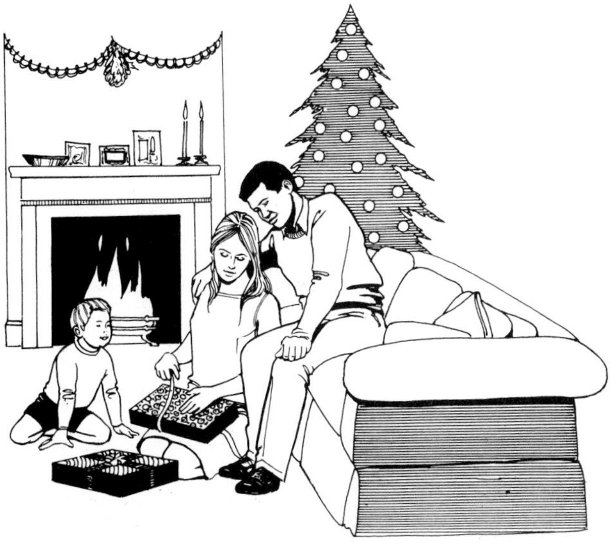

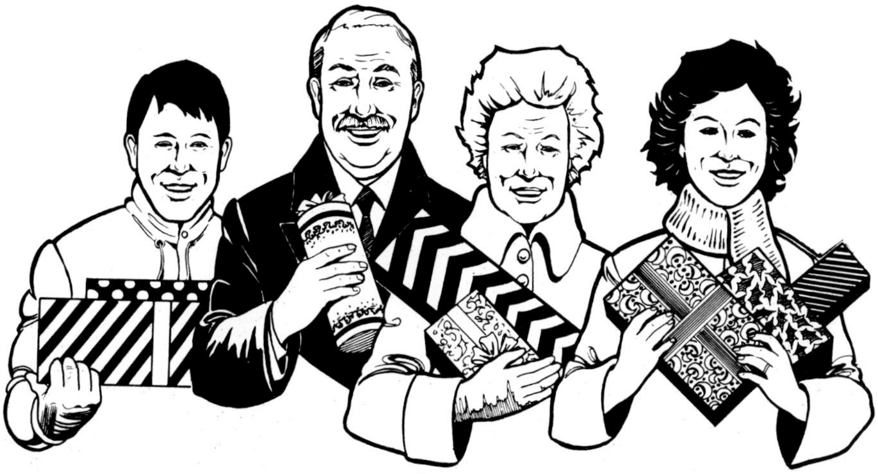

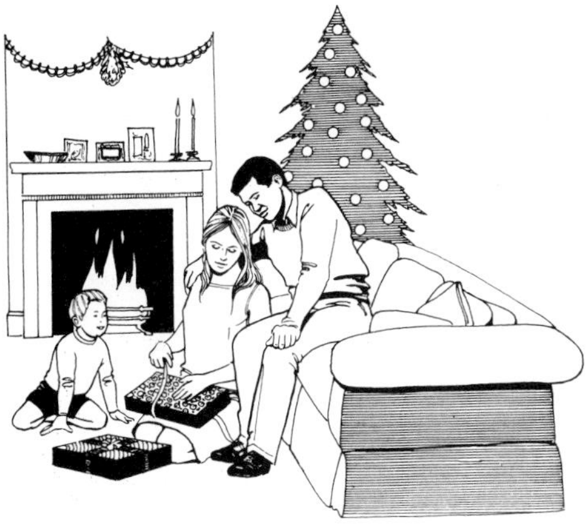

■ Gifts

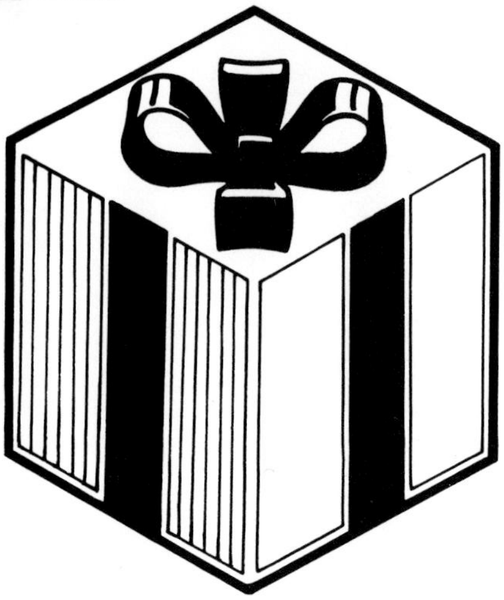

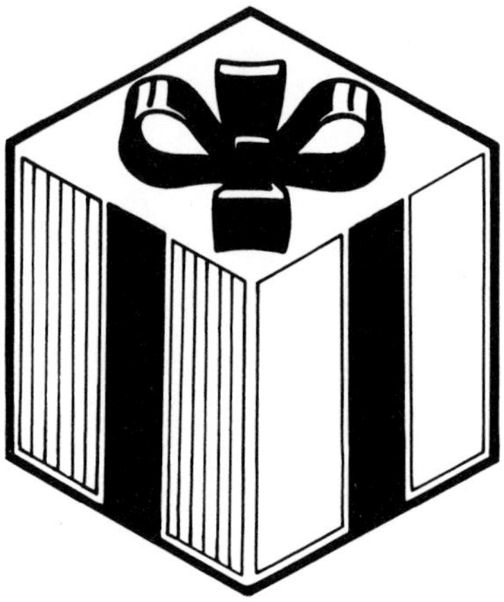

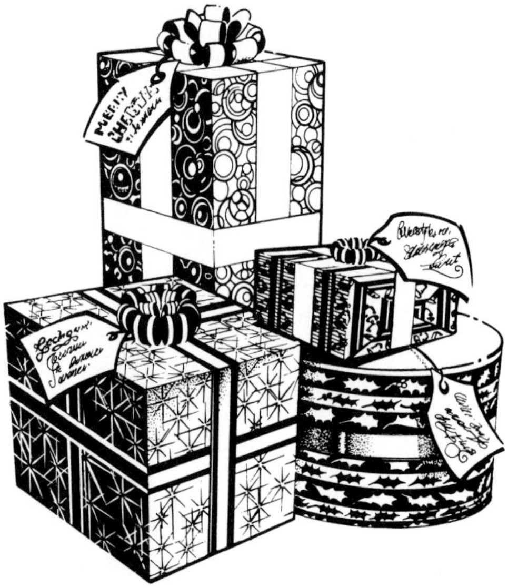

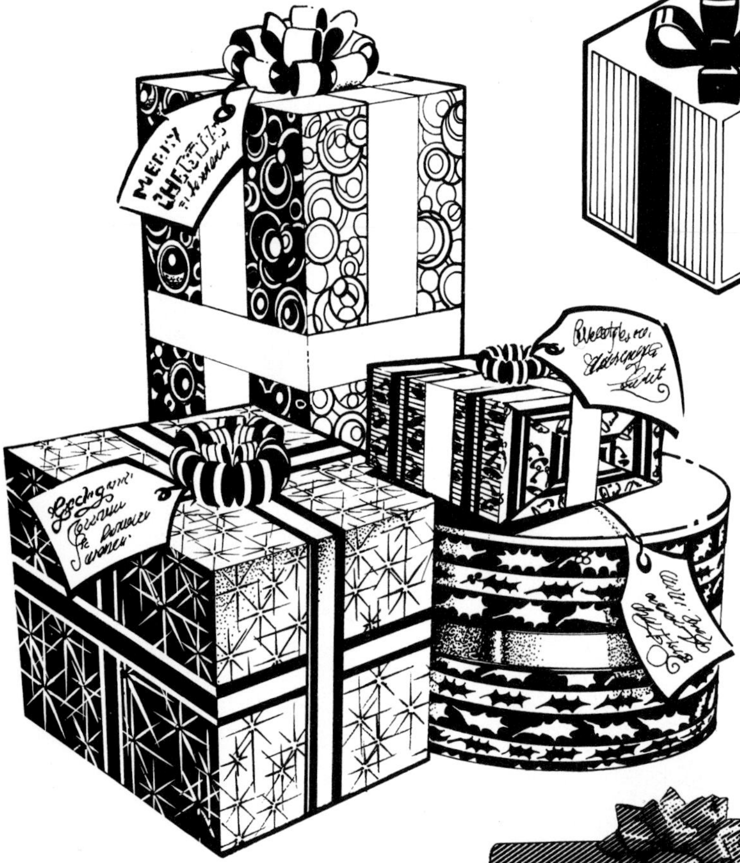

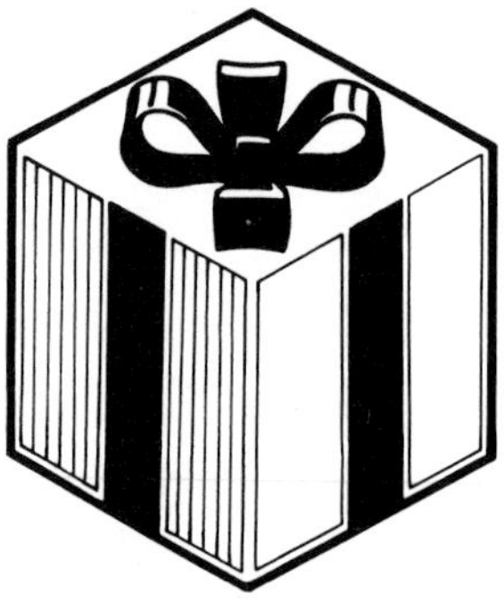

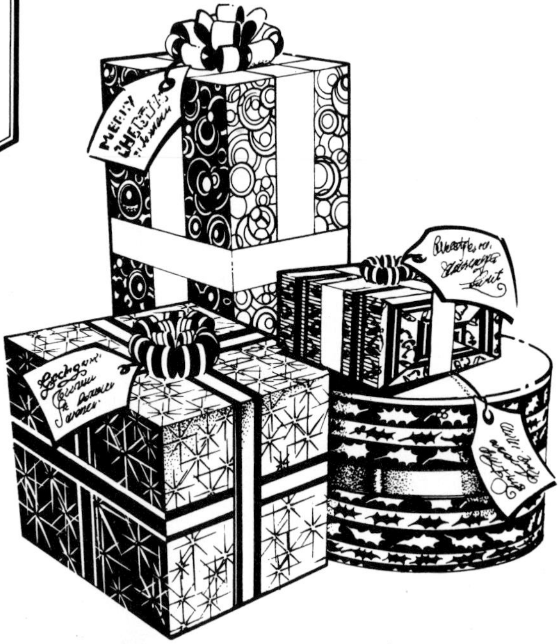

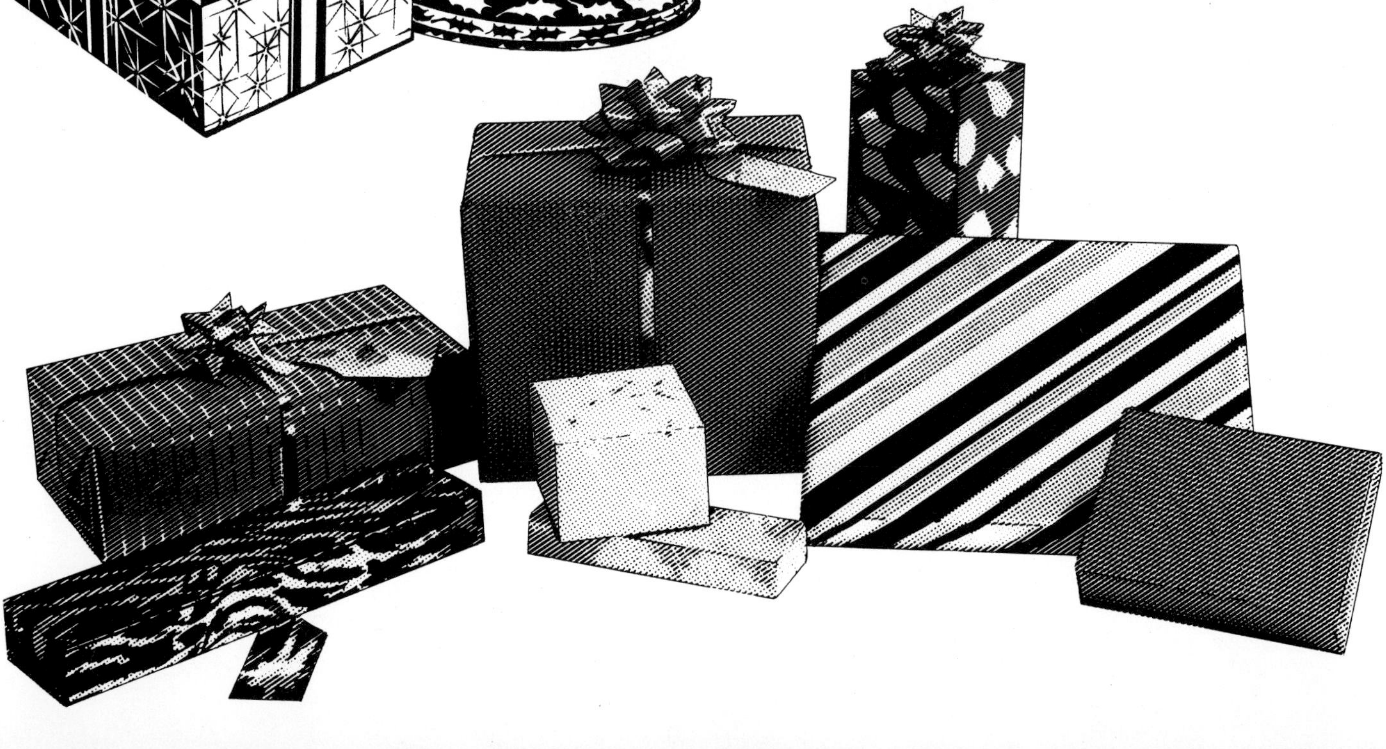

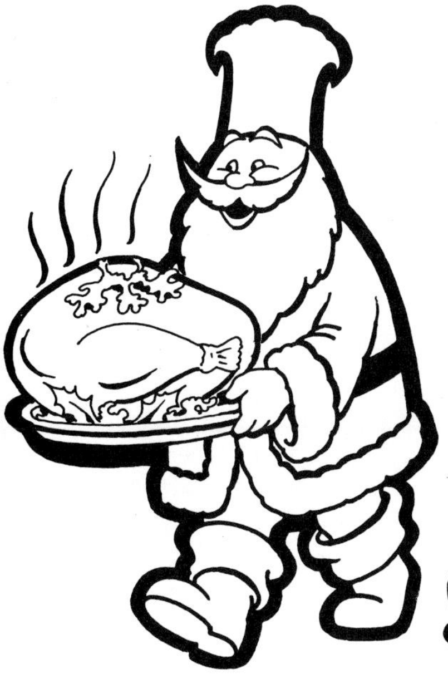

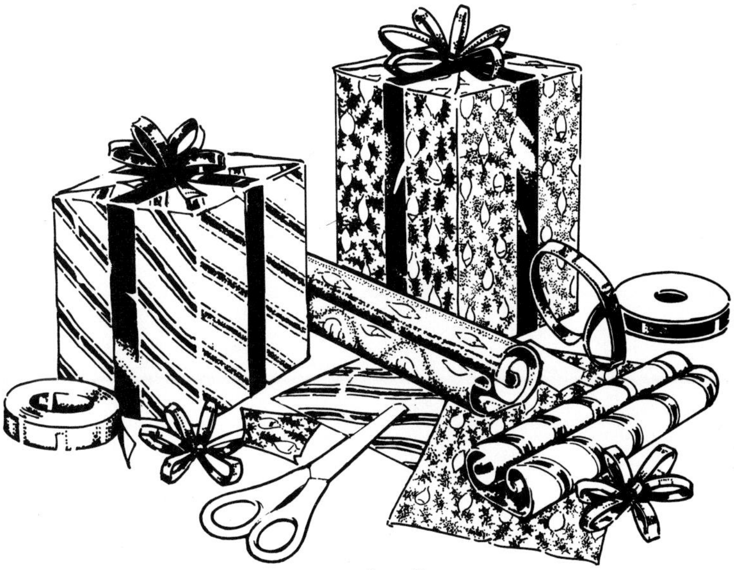

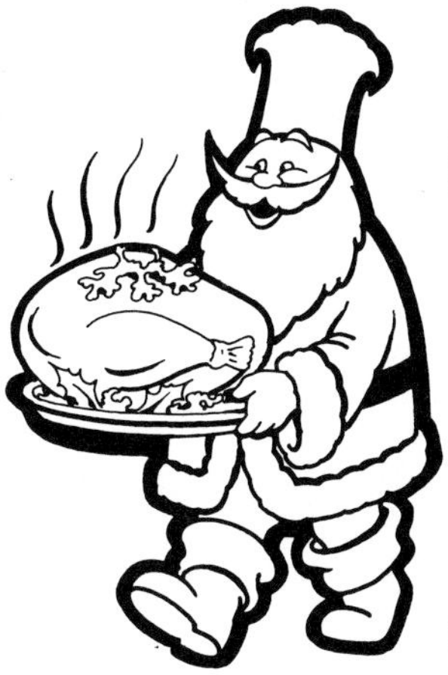

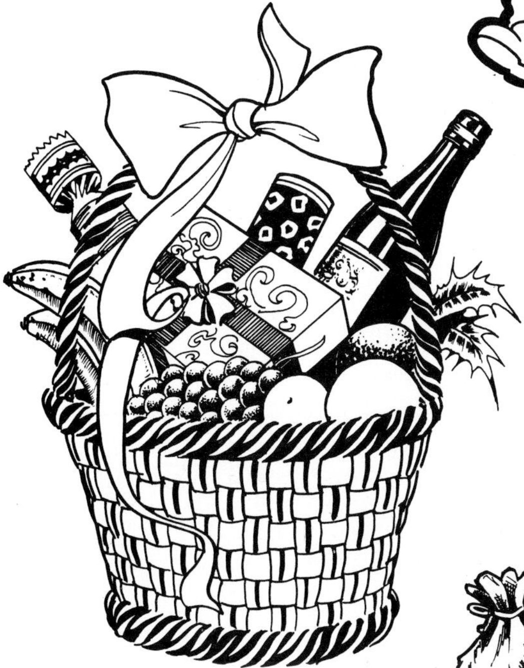

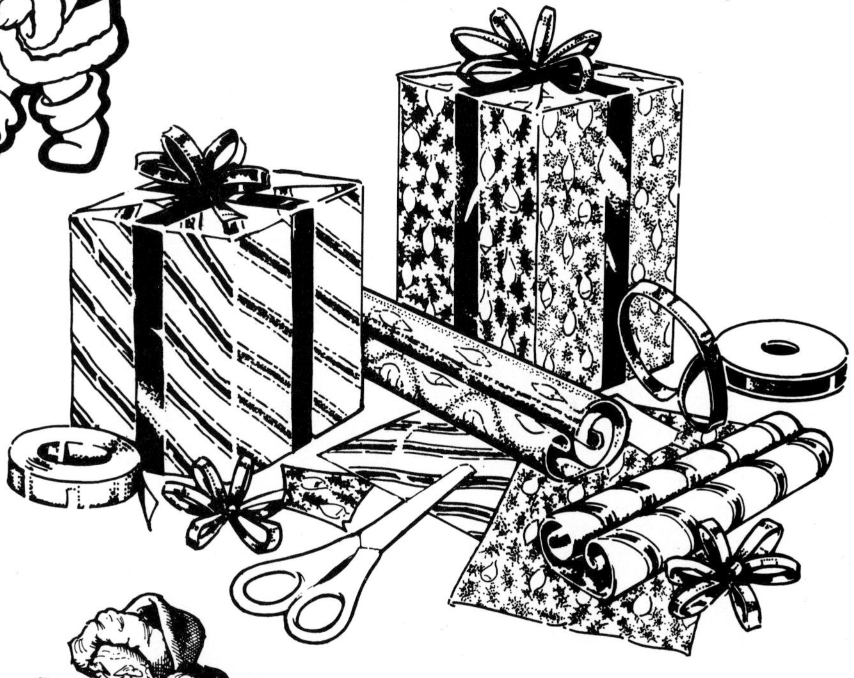

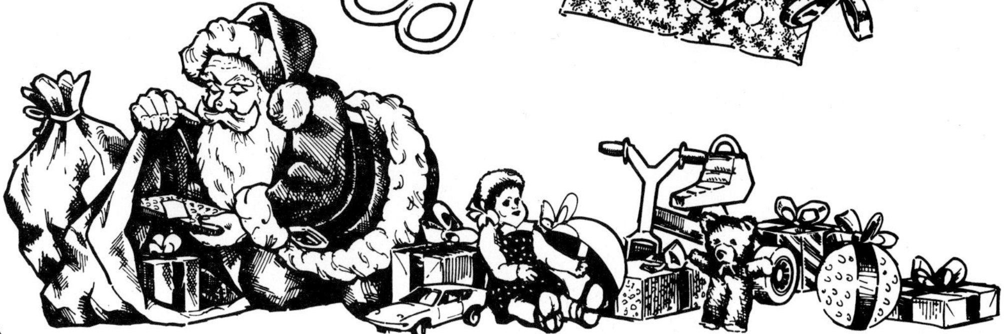

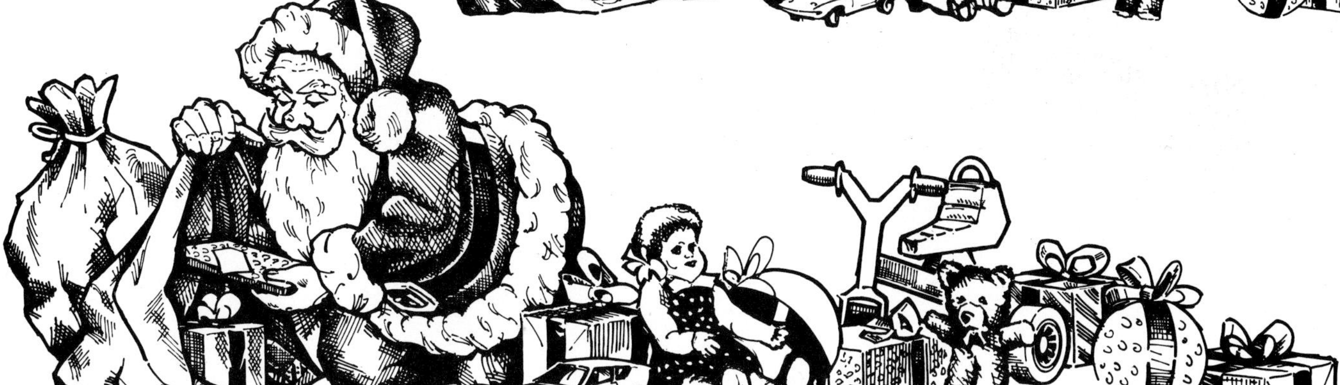

■ Old-Fashioned

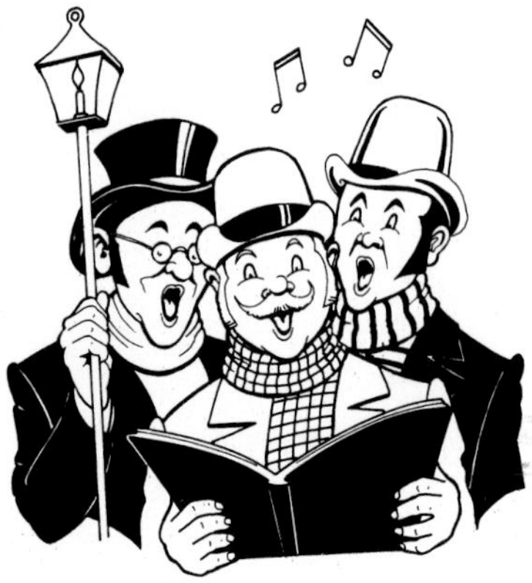

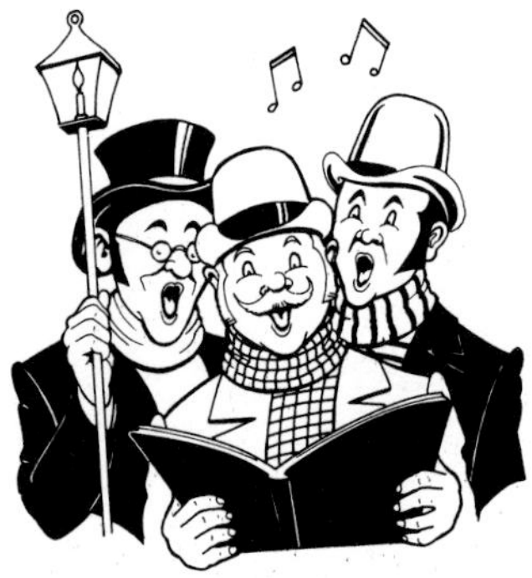

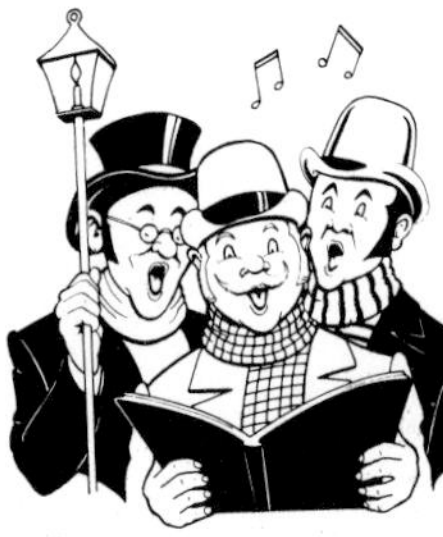

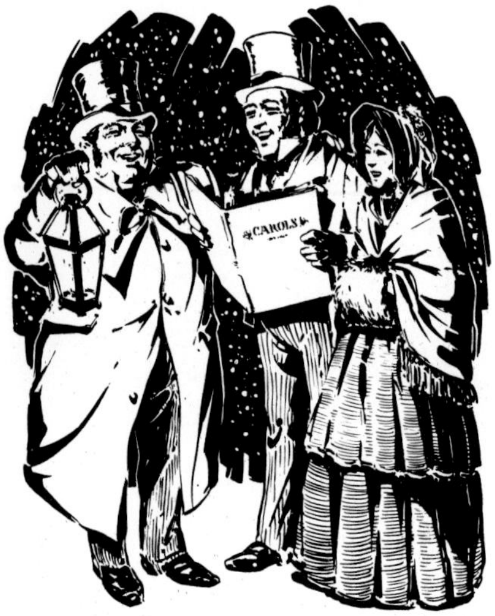

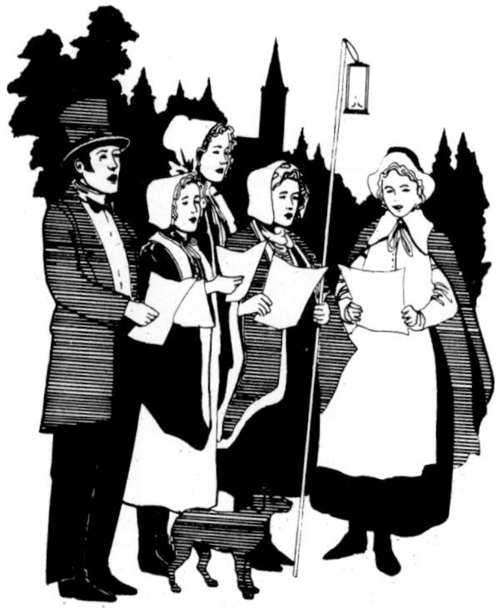

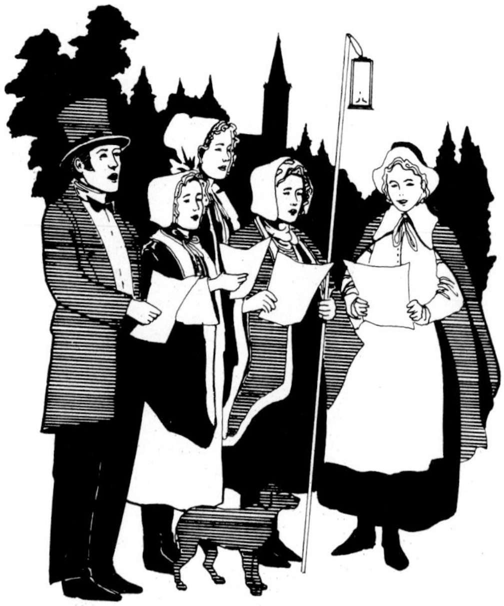

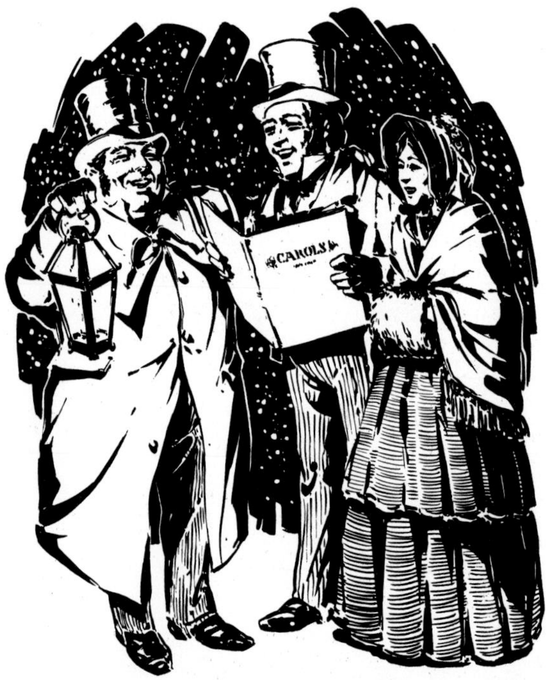

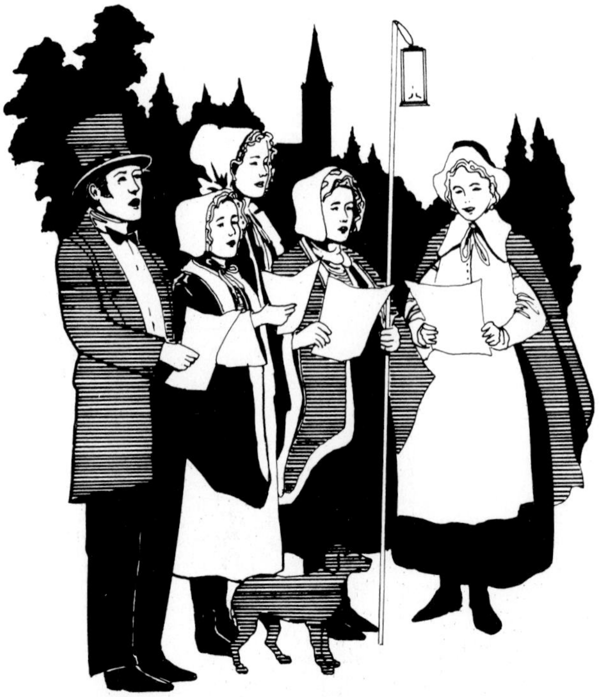

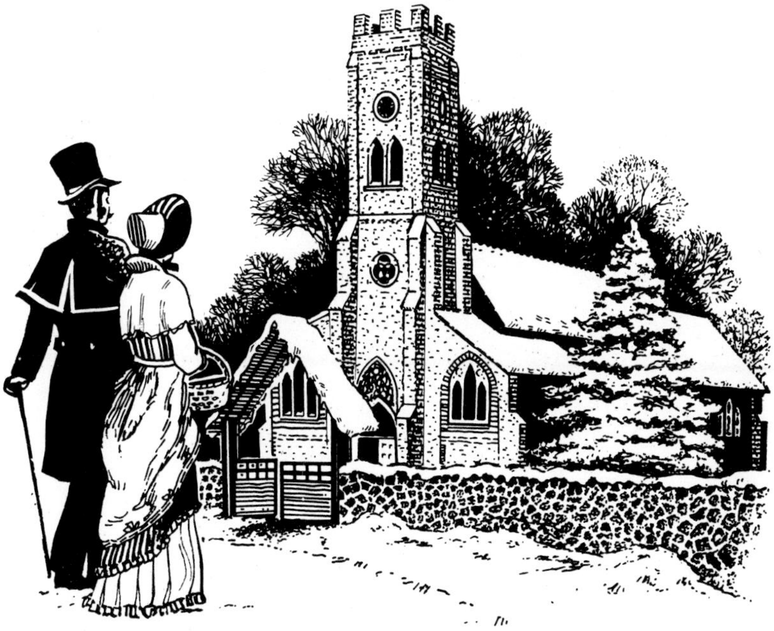

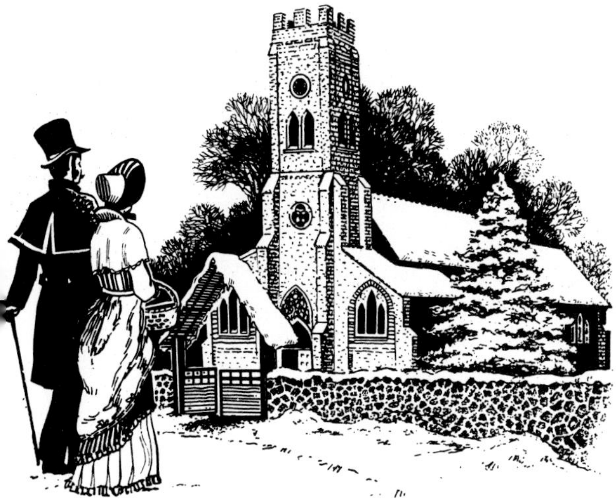

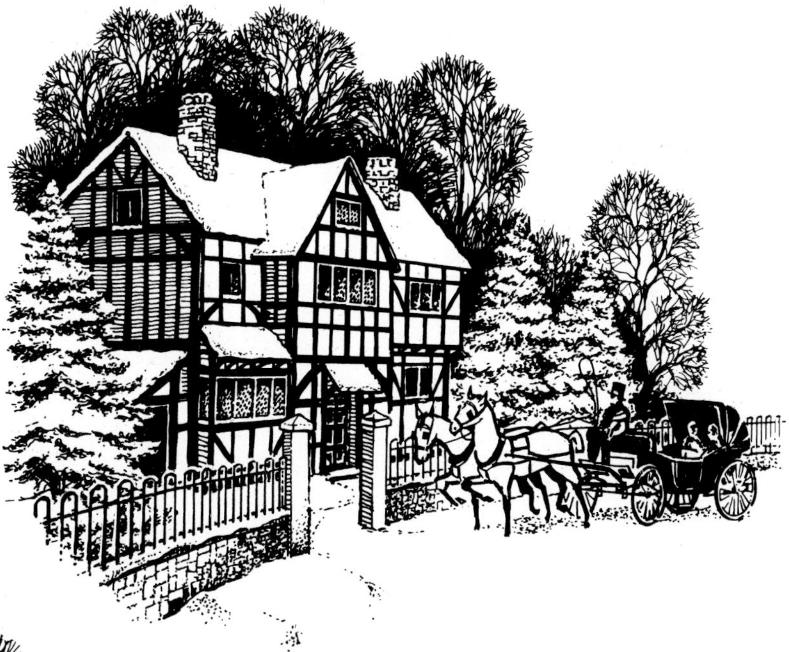

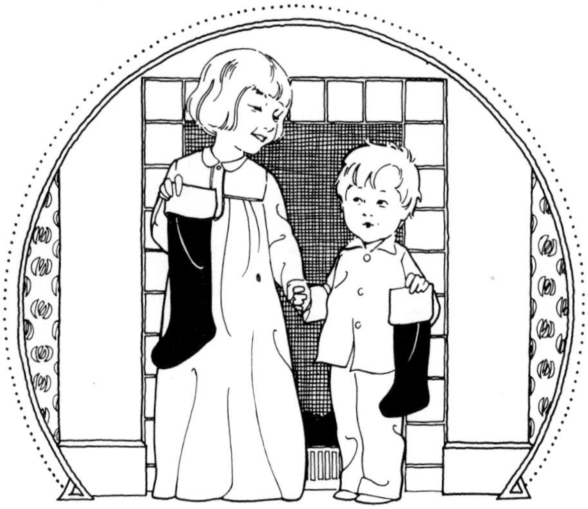

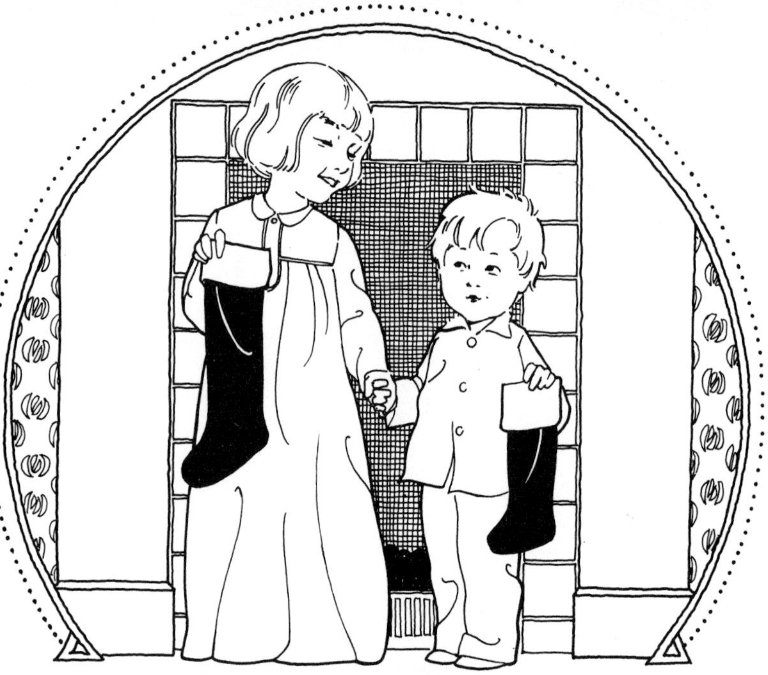

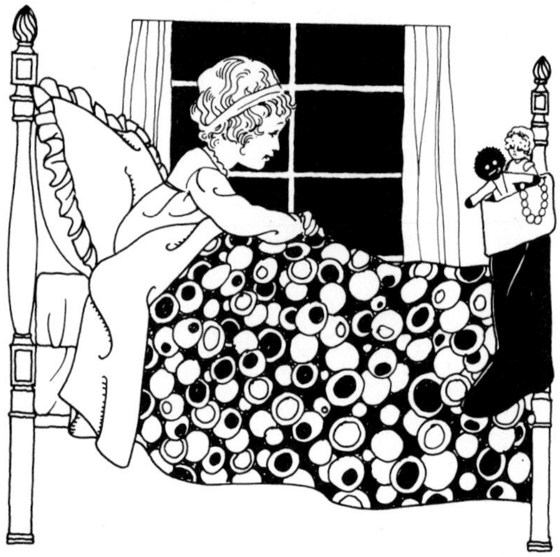

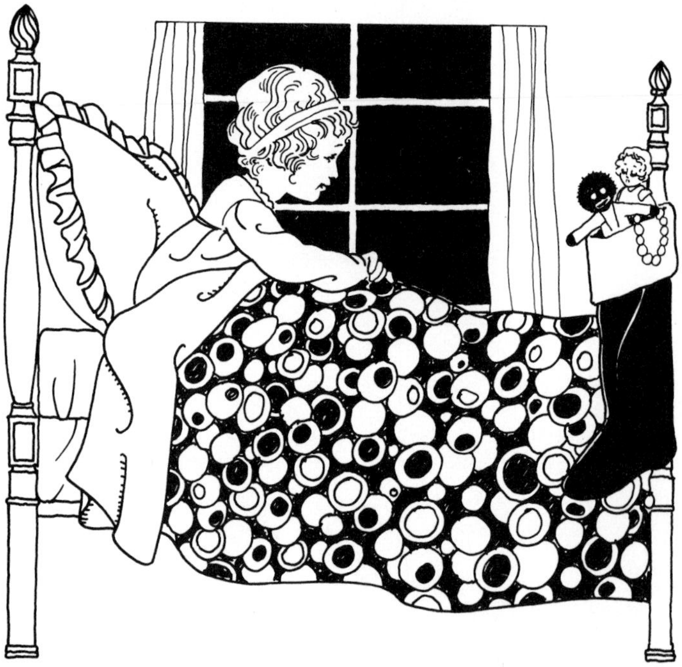

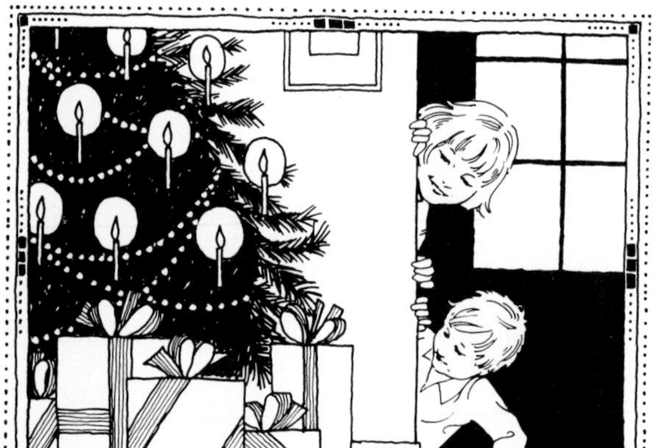

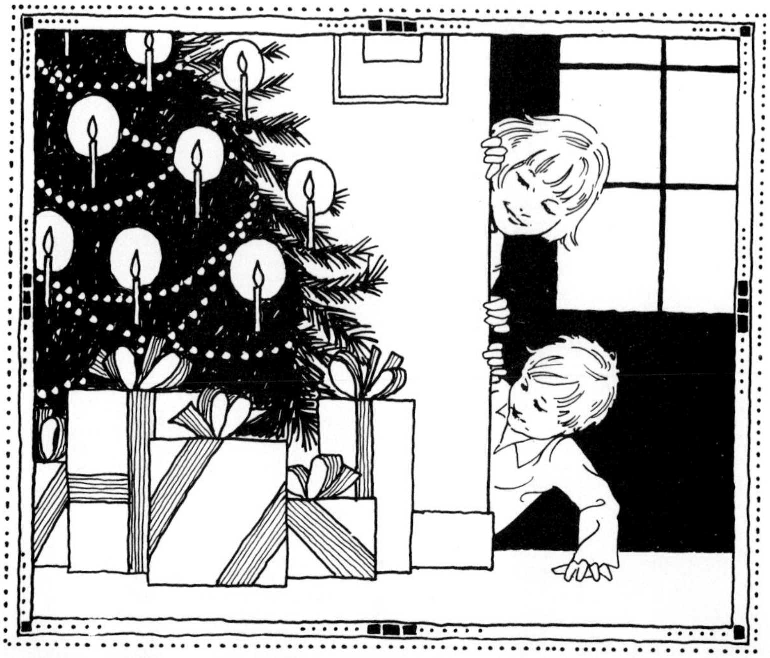

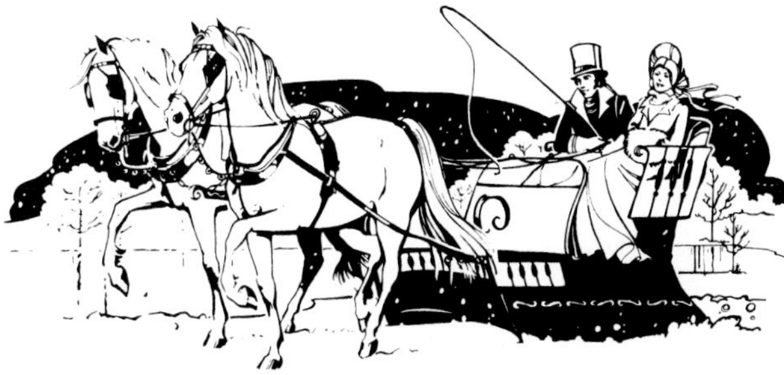

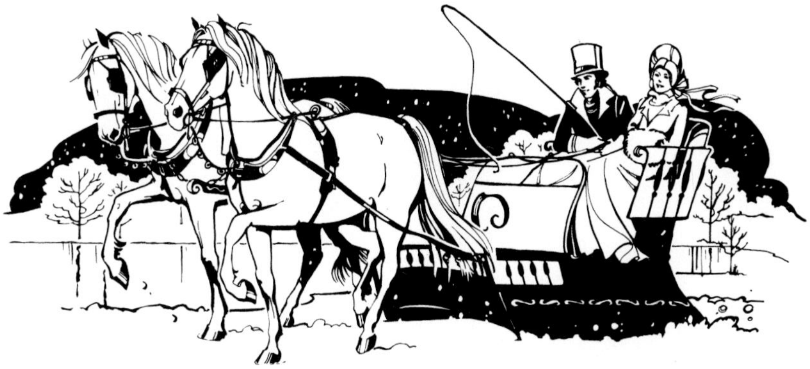

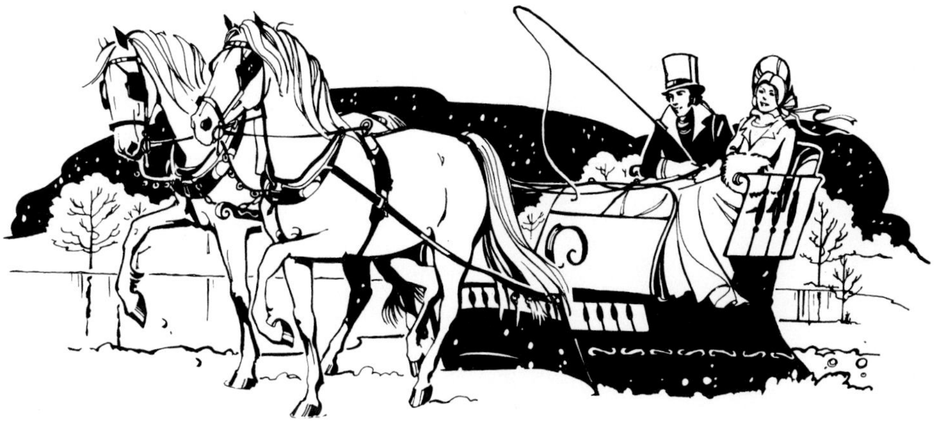

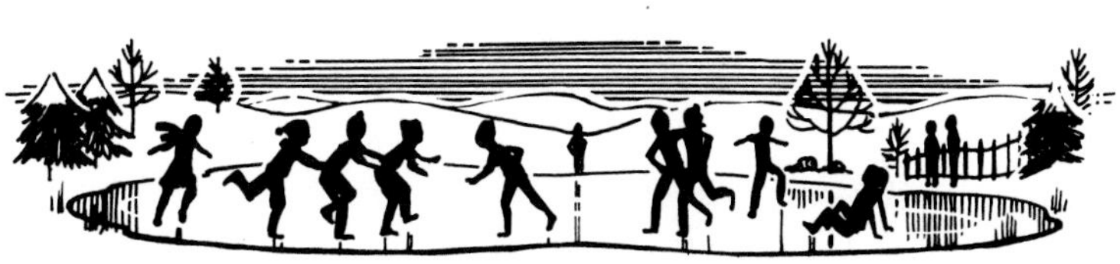

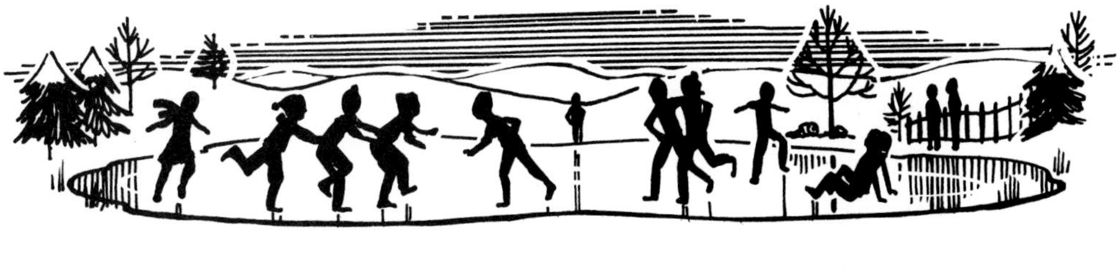

■ Religious

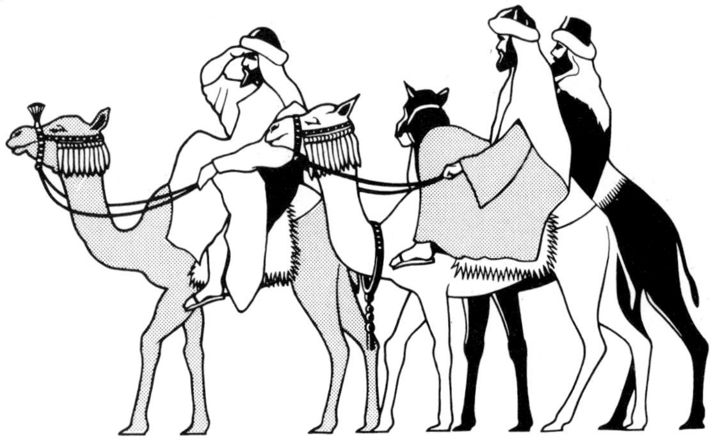

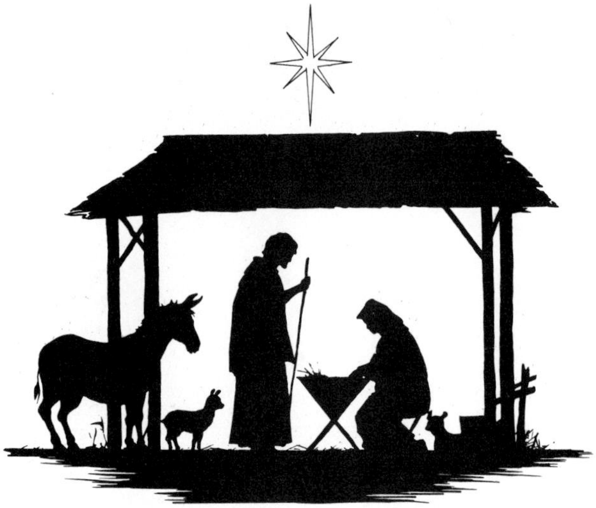

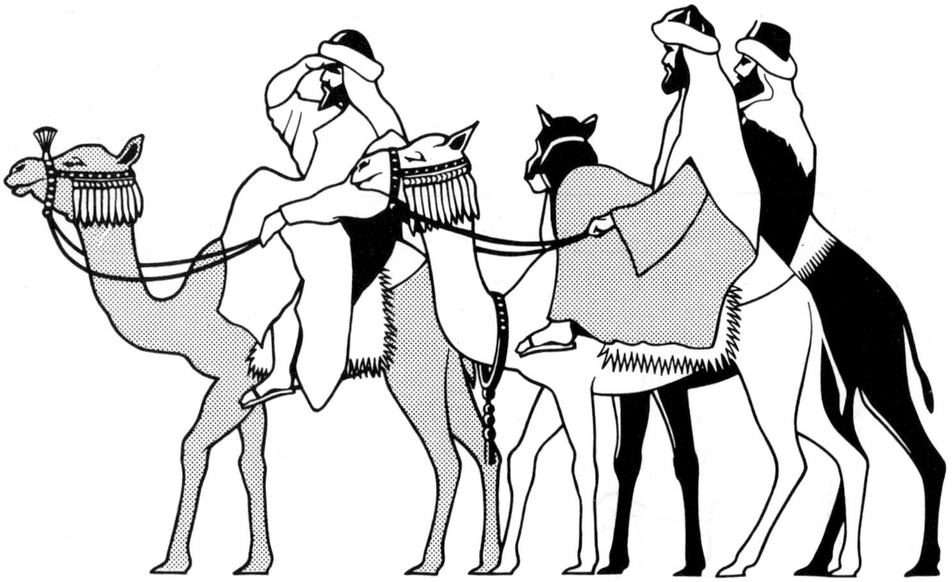

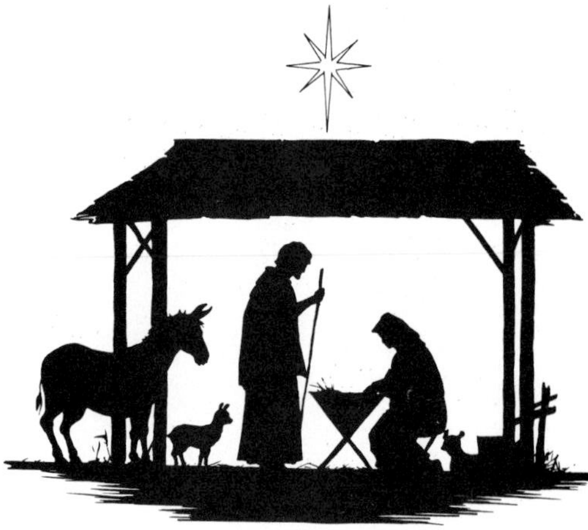

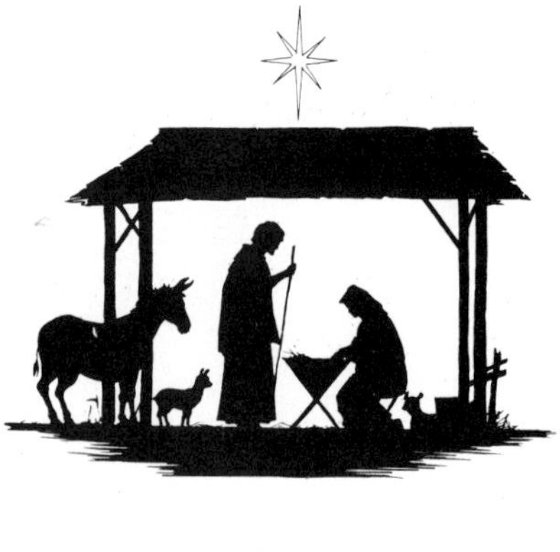

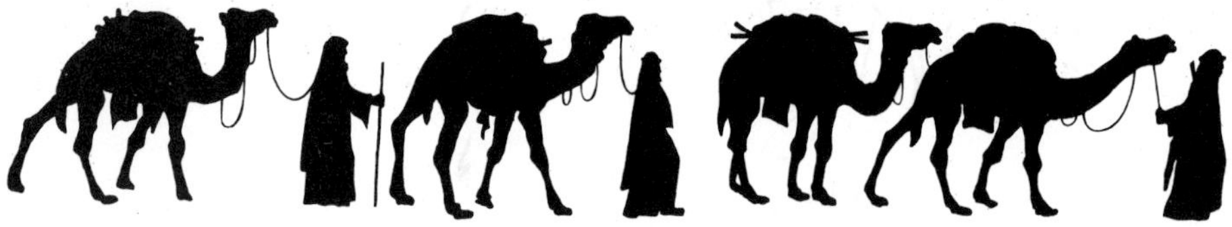

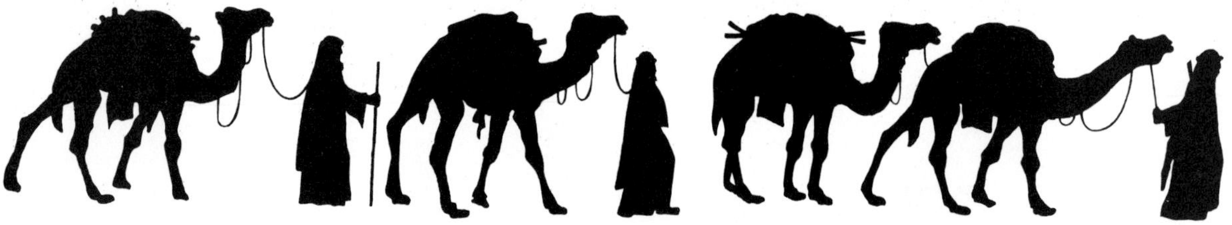

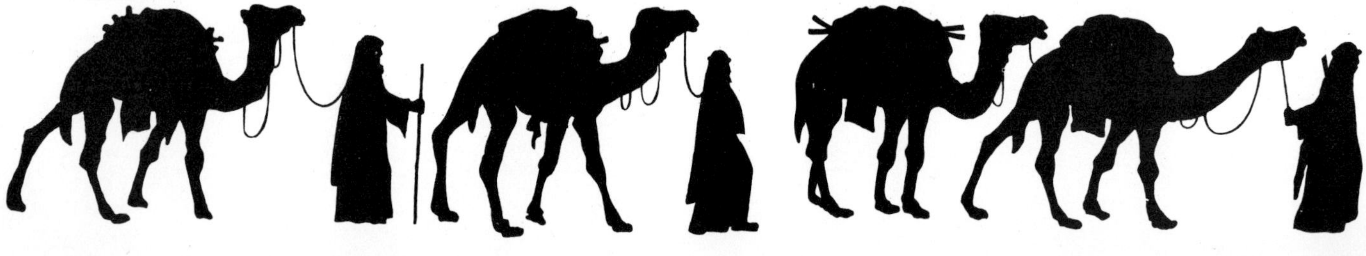

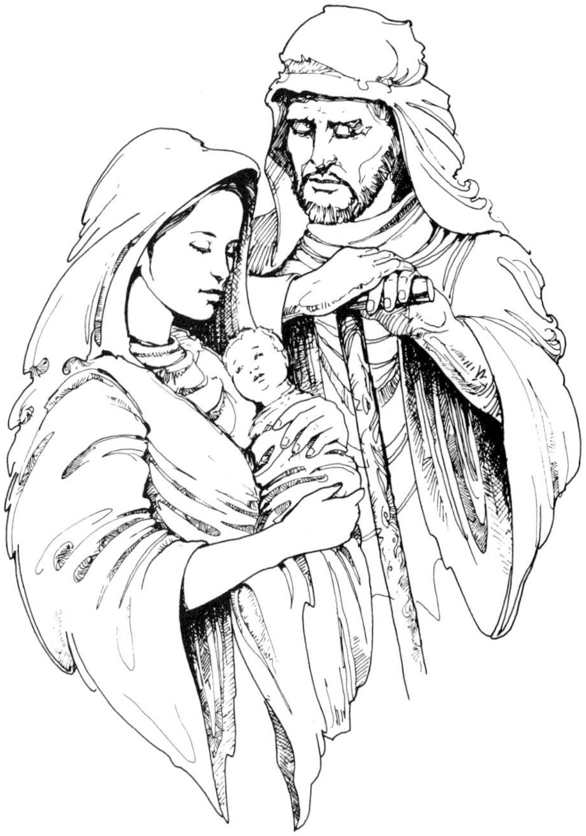

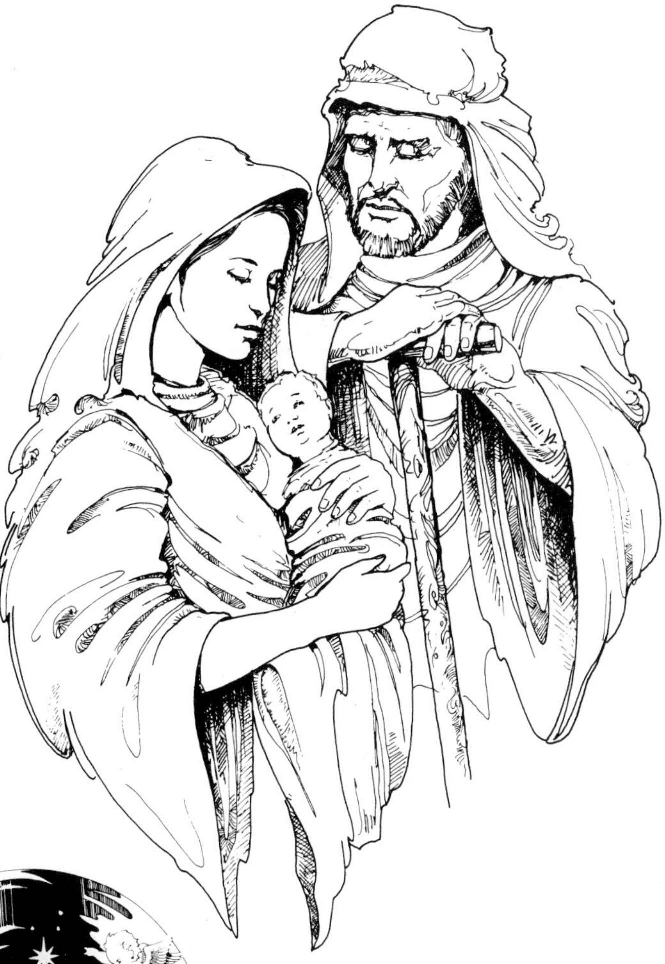

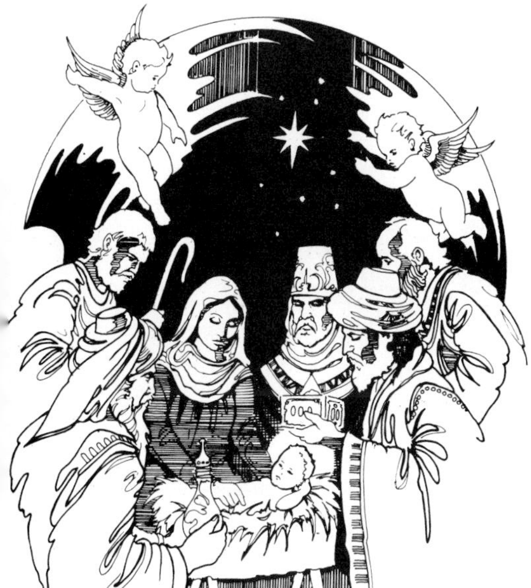

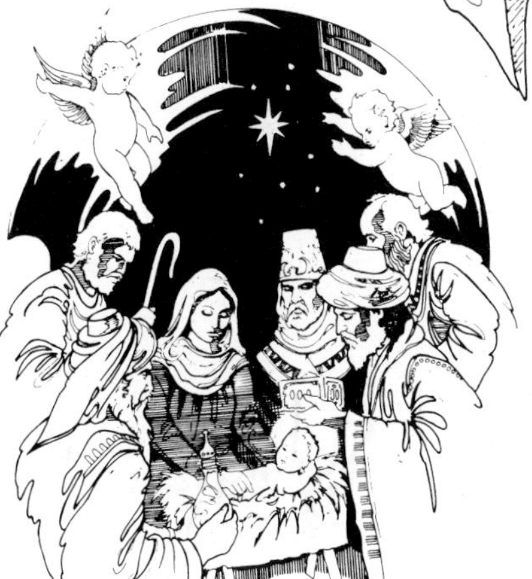

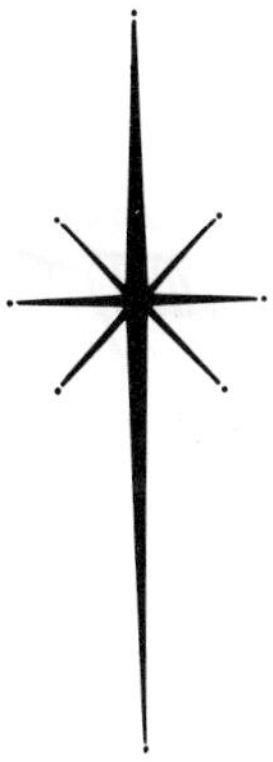

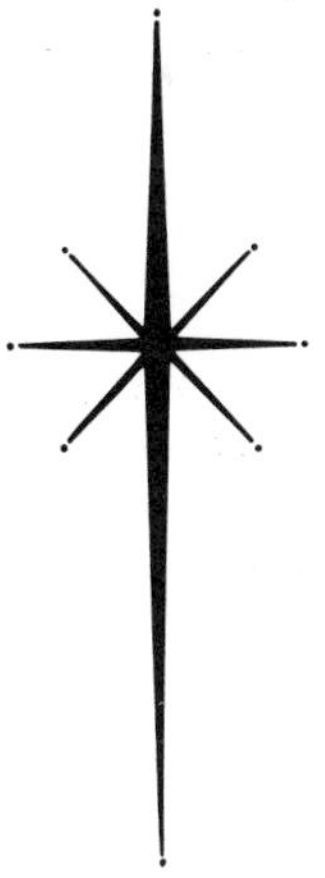

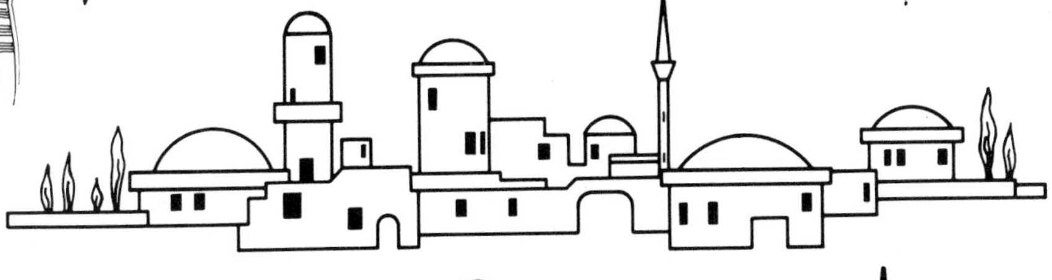

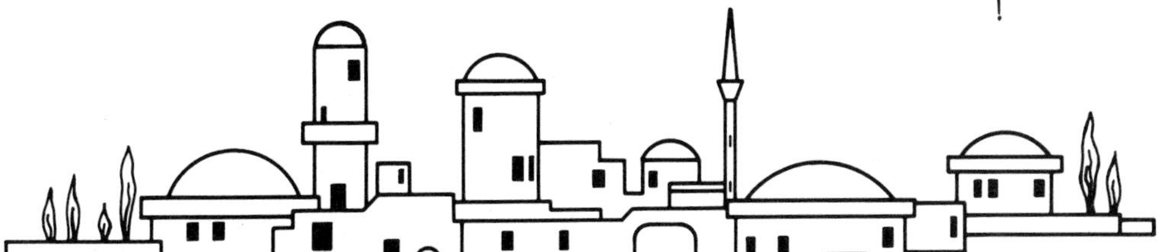

Religious

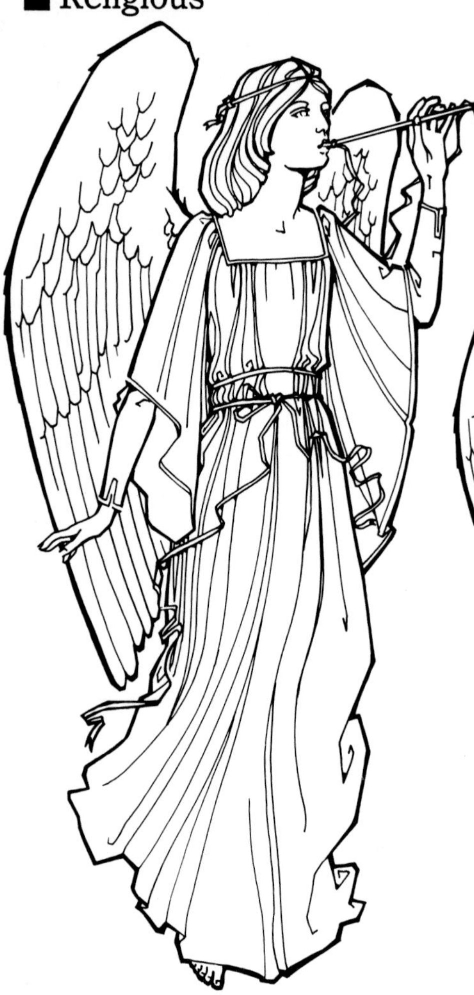

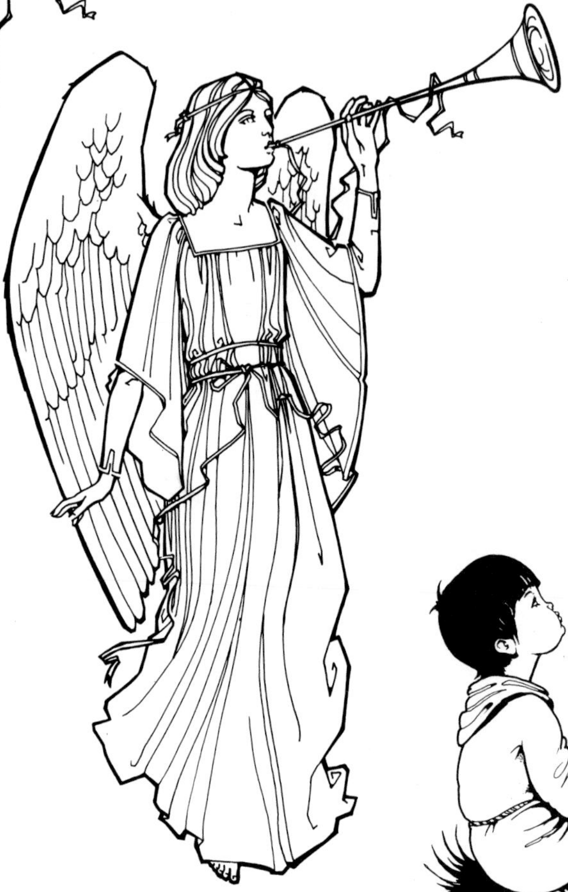

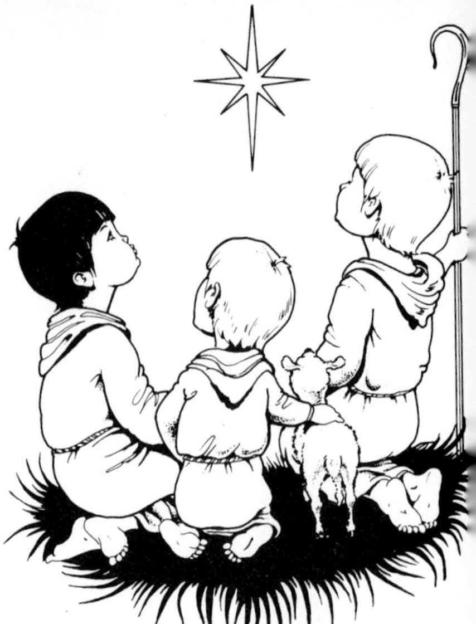

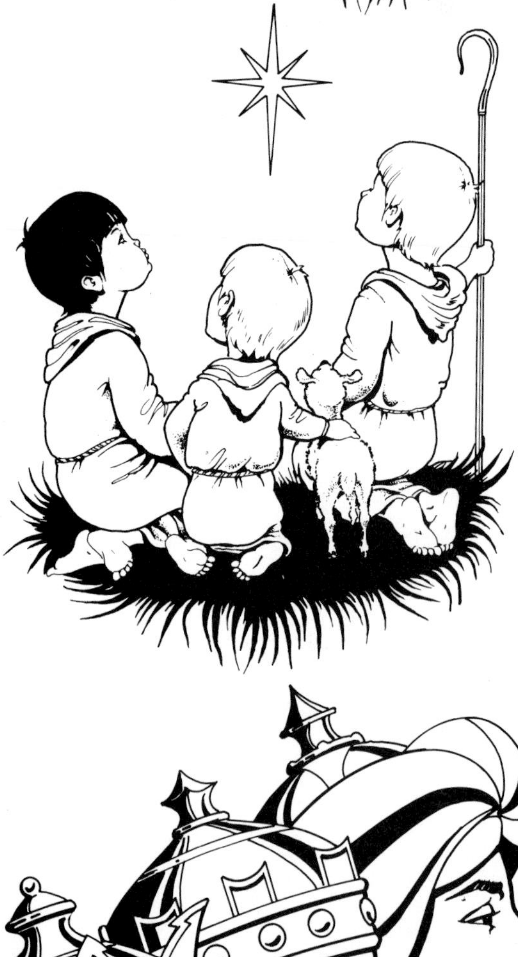

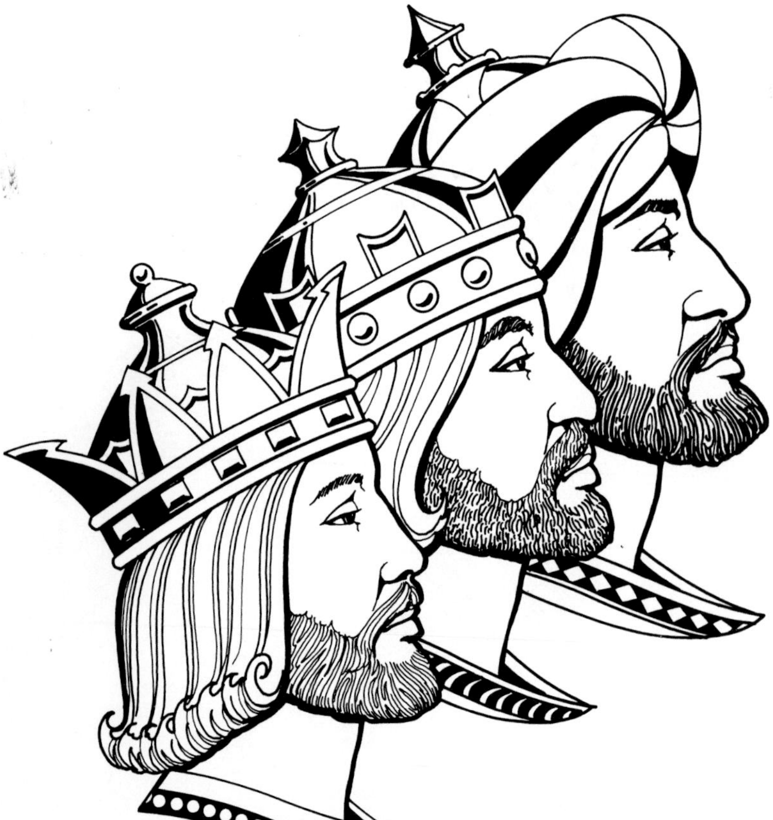

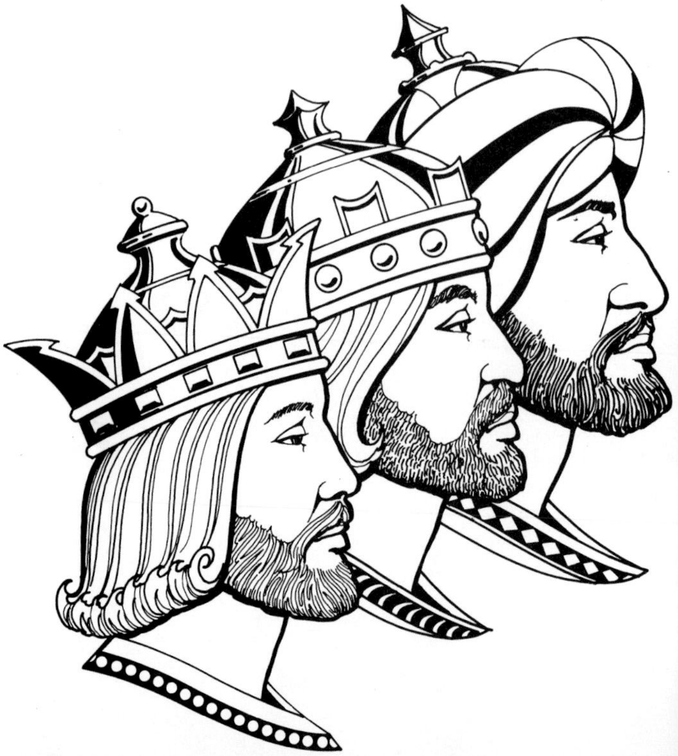

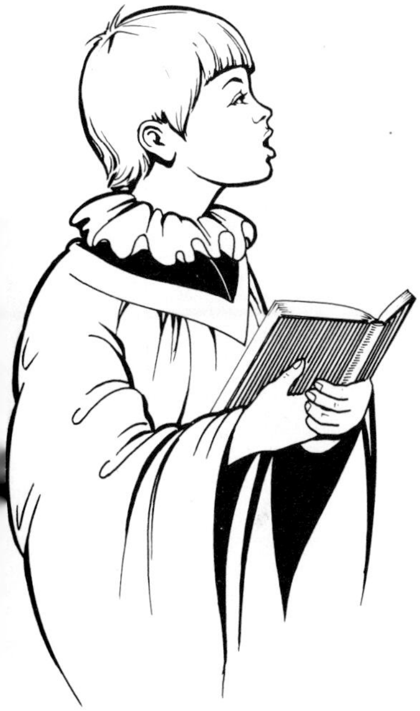

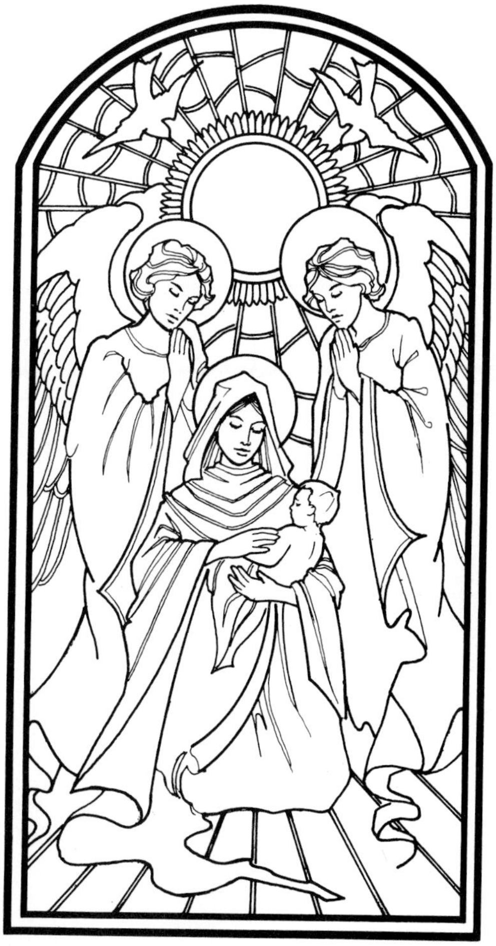

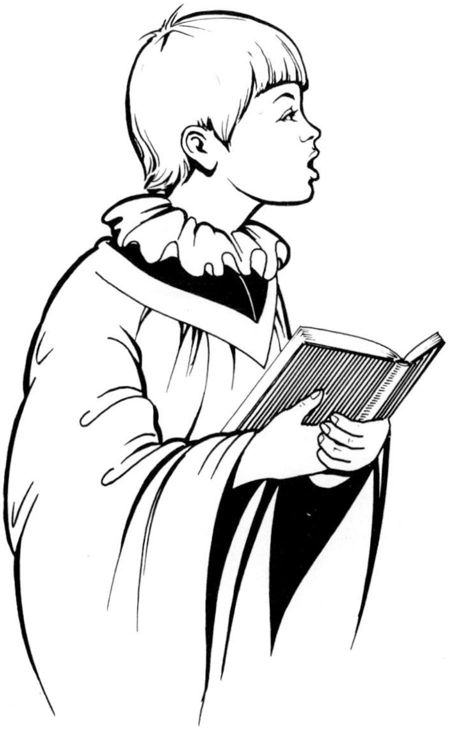

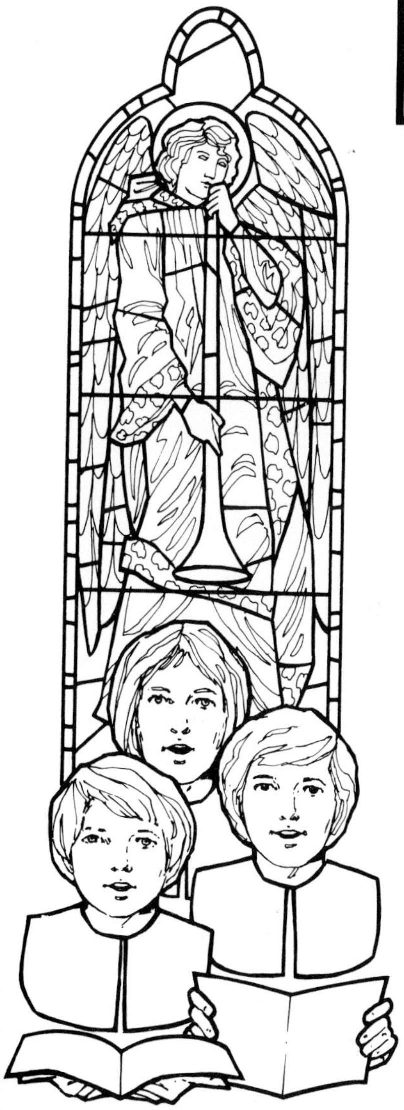

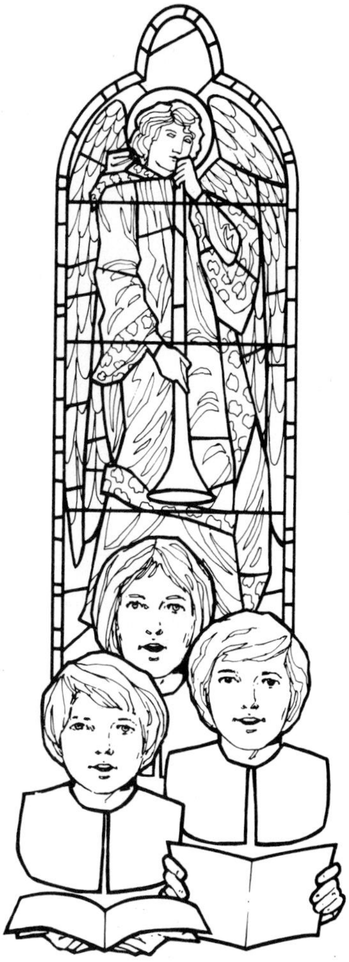

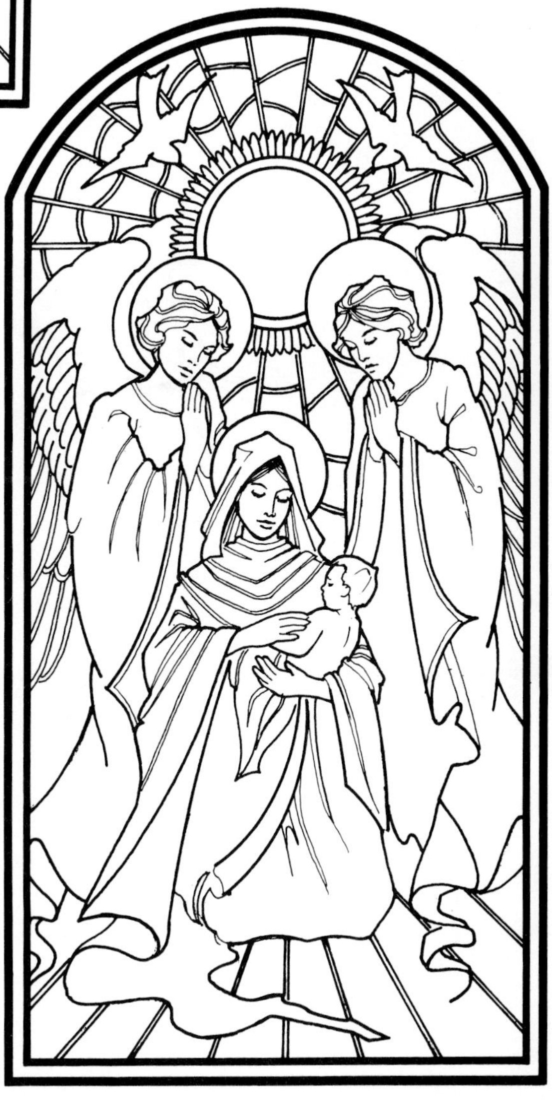

■ Religious

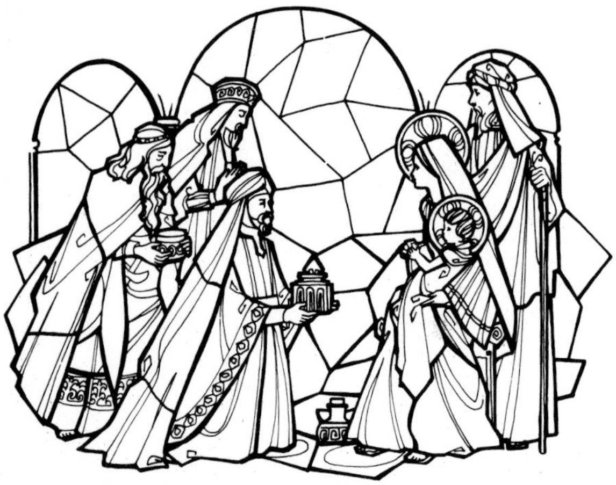

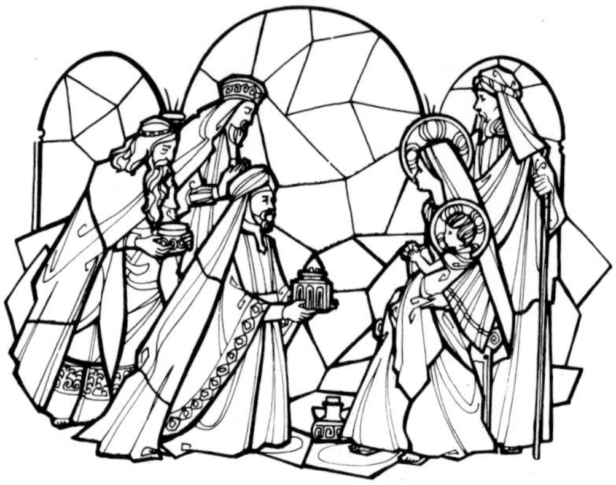

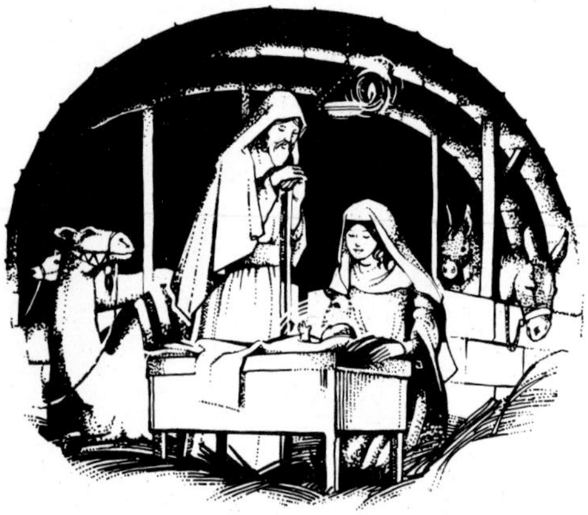

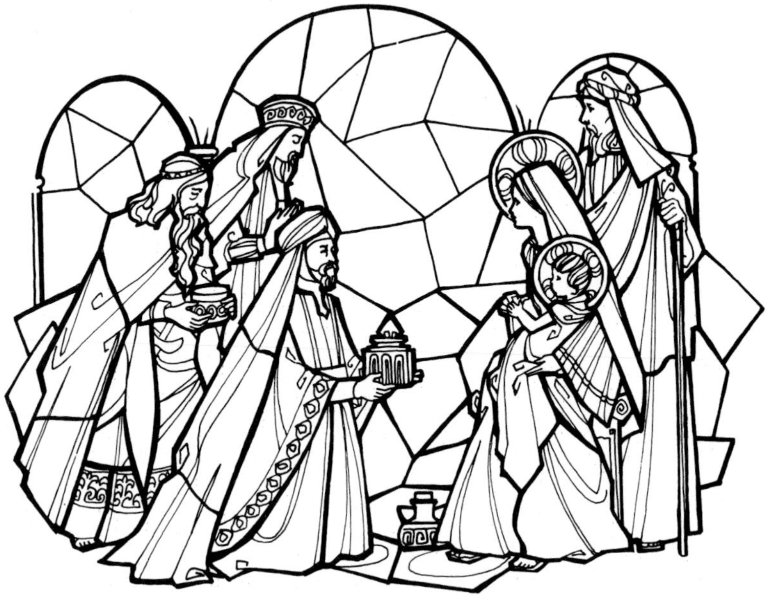

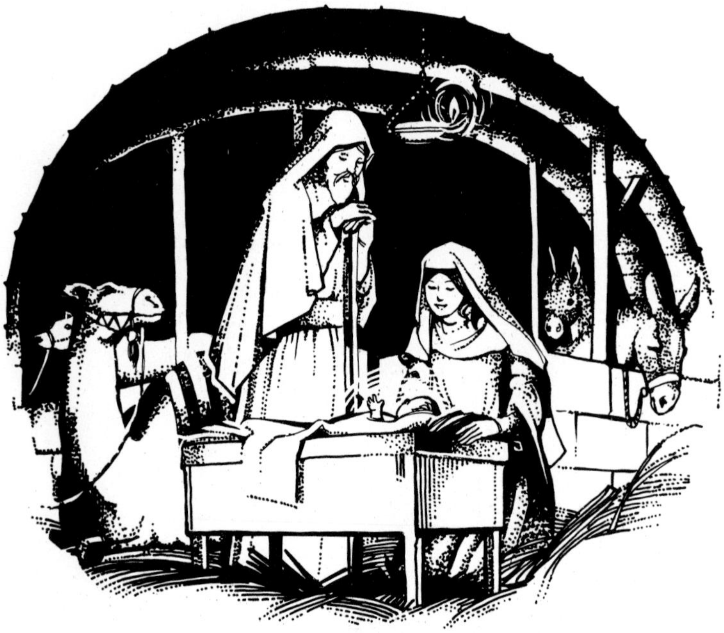

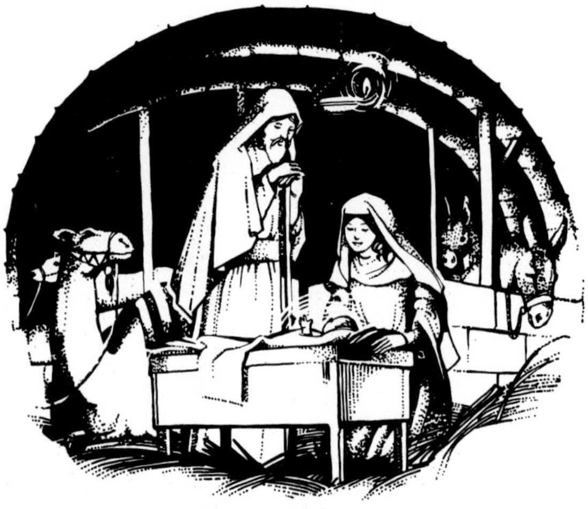

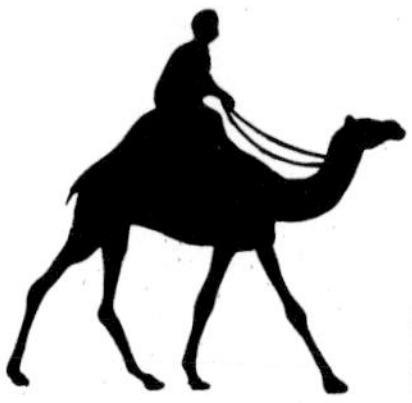

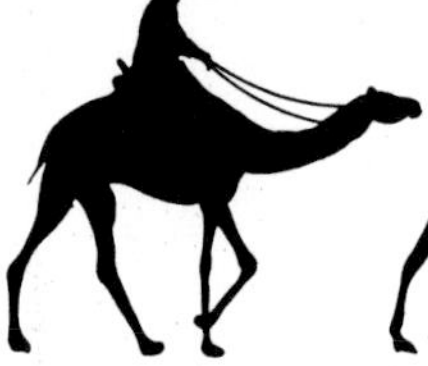

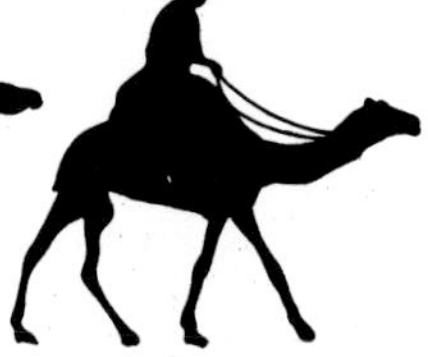

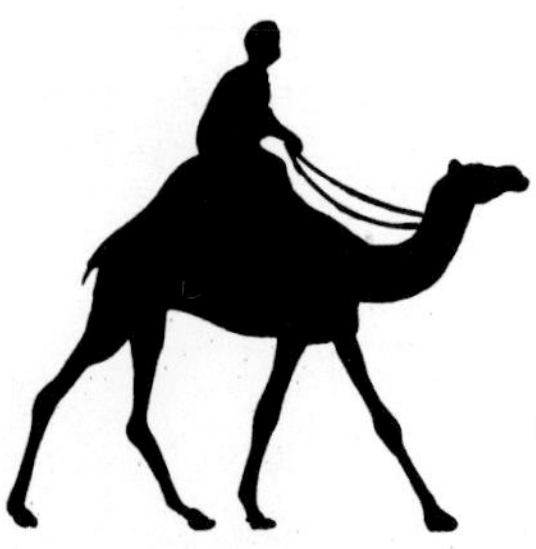

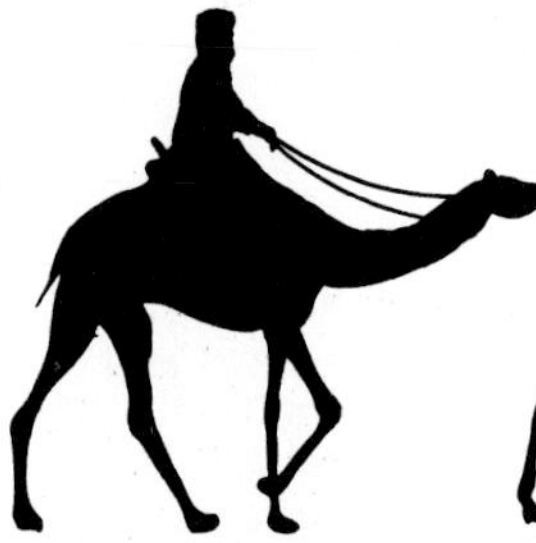

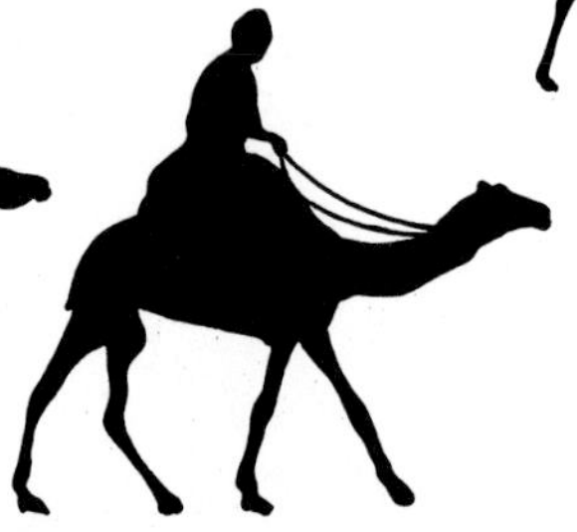

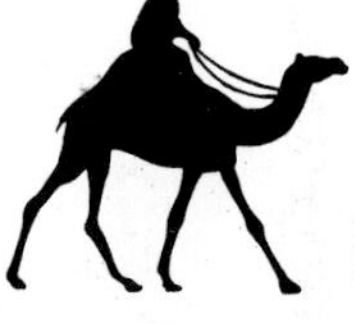

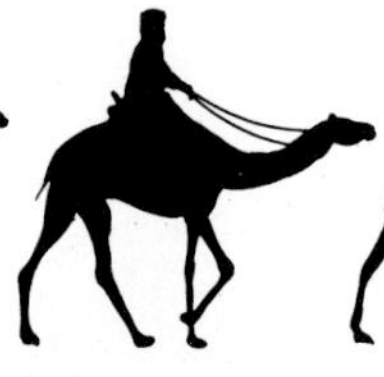

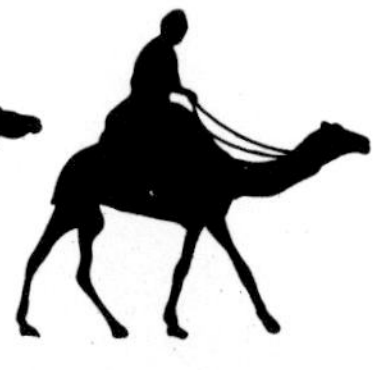